Psychological Dimensions of Executive Coaching

Coaching in Practice series

The aim of this series is to help coaching professionals gain a broader understanding of the challenges and issues they face in coaching, enabling them to make the leap from being 'good-enough' coaches to outstanding ones. This series is an essential aid for both the novice coach eager to learn how to grow a coaching practice, and the more experienced coach looking for new knowledge and strategies. Combining theory with practice, it provides a comprehensive guide to becoming successful in this rapidly expanding profession.

Published and forthcoming titles:

Rogers: *Developing a Coaching Business* (2006)
Hayes: *NLP Coaching*
Hay: *Reflective Practice and Supervision for Coaches*
Vaughan Smith: *Therapist into Coach*

Psychological Dimensions of Executive Coaching

Peter Bluckert

Open University Press

Open University Press
McGraw-Hill Education
McGraw-Hill House
Shoppenhangers Road
Maidenhead
Berkshire
England
SL6 2QL

email: enquiries@openup.co.uk
world wide web: www.openup.co.uk

and Two Penn Plaza, New York, NY 10121–2289, USA

First published 2006

Reprinted 2008, 2009

A catalogue record of this book is available from the British Library

IISBN 10 0335 220 616 (pb) 0335 220622 (hb)
IISBN 13 978 0335 220 618 (pb) 978 0335 220 625 (hb)

Library of Congress Cataloging-in-Publication Data
CIP data applied for

Typeset by YHT Ltd, London
Printed in UK by Bell & Bain Ltd., Glasgow
www.bell-bain.com

The *McGraw·Hill* Companies

In memory of
Alex R. Pannell –
friend and colleague

Contents

Tables and figures

Series preface

The coaching world is expanding. A profession that was largely unknown a decade ago is now an attractive second career for increasing numbers of people looking for new ways of growing their interest in the development of people. Some observers estimate that the number of new coaches joining the market is doubling every year.

Yet while there are many books which cater for the beginner coach, including my own book, also published by Open University Press, *Coaching Skills: A Handbook*, there are relatively few which explore and deepen more specialist aspects of the role. That is the purpose of this series. It is called *Coaching in Practice* because the aim is to unite theory and practice in an accessible way. The books are short, designed to be easily understood without in any way compromising on the integrity of the ideas they explore. All are written by senior coaches with, in every case, many years of hands-on experience.

This series is for you if you are undertaking or completing your coaching training and perhaps in the early stages of the unpredictability, pleasures and dilemmas that working with actual clients brings. Now that you have passed the honeymoon stage, you may have begun to notice the limitations of your approaches and knowledge. You are eager for more information and guidance. You probably know that it is hard to make the leap between being a good-enough coach and an outstanding one. You are thirsty for more help and challenge. You may also be one of the many people still contemplating a career in coaching. If so, these books will give you useful direction on many of the issues which preoccupy, perplex and delight the working coach.

That is where I hope you will find the *Coaching in Practice* series so useful.

You cannot be a successful coach without 'psychological-mindedness', but what is it and can you acquire it? The answer that this simply and directly-written book gives is that yes, you can acquire it, but to do so you need to understand the human response to change as well as the human need for growth and development. As one of our most distinguished thinkers on coaching, Peter Bluckert has written a book that cuts through the confusing thickets of rival psychological schools and gives any practising coach a set of sound guidelines for deepening your understanding of what is really going on between you and your client in a coaching session.

Preface

This book has been a long time in the writing. I suspect that some of my family, friends, colleagues and former students will have wondered whether it would ever appear. I have to confess that I have shared these very same doubts myself at various times. There are some obvious reasons why it's taken so long to complete. Like many of you, I have chosen to lead a fairly busy life and there isn't always time for a book when competing priorities of family, business, friendship and leisure come together. I run a fairly hectic schedule.

Perhaps it's also to do with a sense of identity. I regard myself first and foremost as a practitioner and my sense of satisfaction comes primarily from *doing* the work. Nevertheless, I have always been fascinated by ideas about the nature of human conditioning and how change takes place. These themes have remained with me throughout my life and I have been fortunate enough to come across some wonderful teachers and mentors whose gifts and vision have inspired me. Many of these have come from the worlds of psychology and psychotherapy, in particular Gestalt, which has been my chief psychological frame for many years.

Towards the latter stages of writing this book I discovered another reason for the delay. The simple fact is that it's taken me a long time to know what I really think and want to say about coaching. This shouldn't surprise me given that one of coaching's core propositions is that we don't always know what we think until we take the time to express it to others.

If I have a strong purpose it's to bring together a number of principles and concepts, some of which are fairly simple and others that are undoubtedly complex in a way that helps you make better sense of what coaching is and can be. Because I believe that there are some wonderful ideas out there I make no apology for the fact that I will sometimes point you in the direction of other literature. One of my personal irritations is when coaching authors propound the virtue of learning and then fail to recognise the contributions of fellow writers.

One of the questions I often put to delegates on our advanced coaching programmes is whether coaching really has a theory of its own or whether it is entirely derivative, drawing its thinking from psychology, psychotherapy, organisation development (OD), leadership theory, adult learning, sports psychology and so on. Certainly most coach authors and practitioners reveal a predominant background from one, sometimes two of the following:

psychology, psychotherapy, leadership/management, learning and development or sport.

Because of this array of backgrounds there are many different kinds of coach and approaches to coaching. My own professional background lies mainly in psychotherapy and organisational development. Indeed one of my enduring interests has been to bring some of the insights from psychotherapy, especially Gestalt, into the world of organisation change and development. This has turned out to be no small challenge and to date represents a 25-year journey.

Let me be clear from the outset that I believe certain kinds of coaching require a higher level of psychological competence in the coach. This is not the same as saying that all executive coaches should have a clinical psychology or psychotherapeutic background. Indeed a great deal of coaching, whether undertaken by executive coaches or line managers, is performed by people with little or no psychological training. Mostly, this is absolutely fine and perfectly appropriate, particularly in the case of management coaching. However, all coaches, occasional or full time, know that there are instances when the boundaries of their knowledge, understanding and skill have reached their limits. They feel unsure about what they are dealing with and confused as to why progress is not being made. Some of these situations will probably have a behavioural or attitudinal aspect to them and the seemingly uncoachable individual may be perceived as a problem manager in danger of career derailment. Attempt after attempt may have been made to bring about change and yet nothing seems to have worked. If this scenario rings a bell then this book may help you.

Hopefully it will also make you think in a slightly different way about yourself and the way you work as a coach. I say that because our efforts at facilitating change are often part of the problem, rather than part of the solution. We inadvertently raise resistance to change and produce unnecessary defensiveness through some of our own methods and ways of operating.

Some coaches argue that coaching is a simple process. To an extent I agree. You can learn the basics in a short time. Practising it is anything but. Refraining from telling, solving problems and giving advice is a stretch too far for many coaches. Listening deeply and for long enough to others can be just too taxing, especially when we have our own issues bubbling away. Clients don't always set clear goals, implement their action plans, or leave us feeling good about our work. They get stuck, they feel conflicted and, perhaps most important of all, they often don't really know what they want in the first place.

Then there are those people who have a more complex psychological makeup. They stand out in some way because they either have a lot more of something or a lot less of it. And the rest of us spend lots of time and energy trying to figure out how to work with or around them. This book may give you more of an insight into the ordinary and the less ordinary. You may feel more inclined to take on some of your tougher challenges at the end of it. Alternatively you might give yourself permission to back off and refer on. If you are looking for lines in the sand, which guide you in one direction or the other, you may find some. I genuinely hope so because this work can be difficult. But ultimately there will always be dilemmas and uncertainties. Little is gained without some degree of risk taking.

Who this book is for

My hope is that this book will have a broad appeal across the many groupings that now constitute the emerging coaching profession – executive coaches, occupational psychologists, internal human resources (HR) directors and managers, training and OD consultants, business leaders, and line managers.

It should be especially relevant to those teaching advanced coach training programmes, coaches-in-training and coach practitioners who are looking for psychological understandings to better inform their work. Coach supervisors or therapist/counsellors considering making the transition into executive coaching may also find it helpful.

The structure of the book

What produces successful coaching? Is it about you as the coach – your skills and personal qualities? Is it about the clients – their commitment to the process and motivation to improve or change? Or is it to do with the relationship between you – the vehicle through which learning and change takes place? Perhaps it's about a good coaching process or the fundamental principles upon which coaching is based? If you are looking for some *how to do it*, you'll find my perspective on these issues in Part 1.

Part 2 explores some of the more common themes and issues brought to coaching. Coaching texts often give scant attention to this important subject and this examination of skills/performance, personal development, leadership and meaning-making themes may prove useful to both you as a coach and to your clients, some of whom may not be clear about how best use to their coaching opportunity. The discussion around these four areas will also reveal some of the psychological dimensions to coaching issues.

Part 3 lays some of the foundations for a more psychologically oriented coaching approach and proposes the desirable competencies as well as addressing the training, development and supervision implications. It also looks at four key aspects of coaching sessions: the story, clients' thinking, their feelings in relation to the issue, and the coach's use of self.

The fourth and final part, titled 'Supporting people through change – a Gestalt perspective' is, at the time of writing, the first detailed application of Gestalt to coaching. Whilst Nevis's (1987) book on a Gestalt approach to consultancy stands as the main exposition of Gestalt organisational practice there has, until now, been no significant attempt to set out a Gestalt approach to coaching. Interestingly, Peltier's (2001) excellent book on the psychology of executive coaching, which covers virtually all psychological frameworks from psychodynamic, through cognitive and behavioural, person-centred and even family therapy and hypnotic communication, does not include a chapter on Gestalt. My intention here is to fill this important gap in the literature.

It may be equally important to say what this book doesn't cover. Firstly, it won't be looking at serious psychological disturbance or pathology, and it won't tell you how to diagnose different kinds of personality problems and disorders. Many Masters-level trained therapists and counsellors struggle to do that and it is not a competency that executive coaches can be expected to possess. If coaches are confronted with situations of deeper psychological complexity then they should be guided to stay within their genuine competence and, when appropriate, refer the client on to a clinical practitioner.

Secondly, I am not attempting to cover a wide range of psychological frameworks, models and concepts. This has already been done by Peltier. There are also other psychologically focused management and coaching books that concentrate on particular psychological themes and approaches: Tobias (1990); Czander (1993); Kilburg (2000); Kets de Vries (2001); Greene and Grant (2003); Skiffington and Zeus (2003).

Recurring theme

You will see a recurring theme throughout the book concerning the paramount importance of the self-development of the coach. One of the central messages of this book is that, although tools, techniques and models have a place in coach development, these alone will not be sufficient. On this very important issue I agree with Cason and Jaques (1994) when they say:

> Coaching ultimately depends, for its effectiveness . . . on the level of adult development, of its practitioners. No 'experience' or 'expertise' can make up for the resources a more highly self-developed coach possesses compared to a less self-developed one. If we distinguish between what a person IS and HAS, the latter can be suspended, or left unused. Only the former cannot be withheld and is therefore what really counts.

Acknowledgements

There are a number of people I want to acknowledge for the part they've played in my work and wider life. I'll begin with my work colleagues, many of whom I now consider to be close friends, and a number of my teachers who may not know their considerable impact on my learning and development.

I start with Tina Bain with whom I worked closely for many years and who remains an important family friend. Jane Puddy for her consummate skill, courage and heart. Charley Kreiner for his thinking about and commitment to men's development. Nick Totton for his authenticity and radical stance as a therapist and a person. Annika Giljam for providing excellent supervision and therapeutic guidance.

Alex Pannell, to whom this book is dedicated, and one of my most important teachers as well as close friend and colleague.

My former students and fellow travellers on the Gestalt organisational development programmes and, more recently still, my colleagues, clients and coaches-in-training on our coaching courses have contributed to some profound, sometimes life-changing, learning experiences.

My thanks to Edwin and Sonia Nevis whose influence on my practice has been enormous and for their deep wisdom and goodness about people and change.

Appreciation also goes to Jenny Rogers, the series editor, for her thoughtful, incisive and grounded comments and advice.

Back home I want to thank my parents, Alf and Edna Bluckert, for their constant support and friendship, and Geoff, my brother, for his lifelong encouragement.

Finally to my wonderful family – Lesley my wife, friend and working partner, who has been so much part of developing the thinking and specific ways of working contained in this book. Alex and Louis who warm my heart, make me laugh and, through their own choices, challenges and achievements, provide a constant source of precious moments. Thanks for putting up with me while I've written this book.

Introduction

Delineating the field of coaching

Various authorities have sought to identify the different types of coaching. The European Mentoring and Coaching Council (2006) lists 14 in its report on coaching competencies and standards, and the Executive Coaching Handbook (Executive Coaching Forum 2004) identifies a similar number, which include leadership development, career planning, performance improvement, behavioural change, assessment/feedback processes and presentation/communication skills. The authors of this handbook, an experienced group of US-based coaches, make the important point that executive coaching can involve many of these types of coaching at different times.

Other attempts to delineate the field have produced shorter lists and parcelled the field into management, business, executive and life coaching. This has a certain simplicity and practicality to it. In this schema, *management coaching* refers to line-manager coaching, which, according to a CIPD report (2004), accounts for a significant percentage of overall coaching delivered within UK companies.

Business coaching is a more generic term and refers to any coaching activity that takes place in an organisational setting. In that sense, it isn't confined to working with executives, senior managers or business owners. Many aspiring coaches have yet to acquire executive clients and may not wish to do so. The term 'business coach' is therefore more fitting. Internal HR coaching, where it is neither executive nor line focused, could also be more accurately described as business coaching. It can encompass everything from leadership development to skills coaching and may also have a more strategic focus such as business planning, or facilitating a more performance-focused organisational culture.

Executive coaching is interpreted in different ways. Some define it as a personalised learning and development process designed to improve the performance of executives. Others ascribe a more technical meaning within the broader field of organisational consultation and highlight the behavioural change aspect. From this perspective executive coaches are not simply people who work with executives – they are behaviourally trained practitioners working with a distinctive methodology.

Life coaching is an activity that attempts to support people wishing to make some sort of significant change in their lives. It often starts with questions about what clients really want from their lives and whether they are living their best life. It involves clarifying values, establishing a vision and setting stretching goals to achieve a more personally satisfying and fulfilling life.

Towards a definition of coaching

Definitions of coaching mainly group around learning and development linked to performance improvement and coaching to facilitate personal growth and change. The particular emphasis reflects the professional background of the coach/author. A significant number of academics and individuals from HR, consultancy and OD focus on learning and development. Those from results-oriented environments such as sports and business tend to concentrate on the performance theme and see coaching as being about skills development. Behavioural coaches, coaching psychologists, counsellors and therapists generally define coaching in terms of change.

There can be little argument with a process that promises to deliver learning and development, especially when it is said to produce improved effectiveness and performance. Most of us are relatively comfortable with the concepts of learning and development – they have a feel-good factor about them. This may not always be the case when defining coaching in terms of change. We can be touchier about the notion that there are aspects of ourselves that require attention, whether those relate to our thinking, our emotional self-management or our behaviours. Nevertheless, there are many in the coaching field who define coaching predominantly in these terms.

The behavioural-change focus of coaching is one of the key differentiators from those who come from the learning and development modality; this is where the psychological agenda more strongly enters the frame. Those who emphasise behavioural change as the dominant focus come from business or clinical psychology, psychotherapy and counselling or have added some element of psychological training such as psychometric assessment to their previous professional background.

Kilburg (2000) provides one of the most quoted definitions of executive coaching:

> ...a helping relationship formed between a client who has managerial authority and responsibility in an organisation and a consultant who uses a wide variety of behavioural techniques and methods to assist the client to achieve a mutually identified set of goals to improve his or her professional performance and personal satisfaction and consequently to improve the effectiveness of the client's organisation within a formally defined coaching agreement.

Similar themes are echoed in Grant's (2003) view that 'the coaching process should be a systematic, goal-directed process to facilitate sustained change' and Zeus and Skiffington's (2000) position: 'Executive coaching is a collaborative, individualised relationship between an executive and a coach, the aims of which are to bring about sustained behavioural change and to transform the quality of the executive's working and personal life.'

My own preference is for a broad-based definition of coaching because it keeps options open and reflects the reality of my own coaching experience. In the world of business, for coaching to be seen as relevant and a positive intervention, it must go beyond the facilitation of learning and development and directly translate into more effective action and improved performance. It must also embrace the personal change agenda, especially when behaviours have been identified as problematic. With these factors in mind, I define coaching as follows: 'Coaching is the facilitation of learning and development with the purpose of improving performance and enhancing effective action, goal achievement and personal satisfaction. It invariably involves growth and change, whether that is in perspective, attitude or behaviour.'

In reviewing this definition, you will notice that it encompasses personal satisfaction and growth. Some years ago, personal satisfaction would not have made the starting line. The focus would have been entirely on what coaching enables the individual to do for the organisation's benefit. However, there is now a greater acknowledgment and acceptance that a person's wellbeing, motivation and happiness at work is not just morally desirable but also makes sound, economic sense. There needs to be a decent deal for both sides otherwise successful, highly competent people leave to find it elsewhere. Growth is an evocative concept and difficult to define, yet it's fundamental to coaching because it refers to that most compelling of coaching notions – that coaches are there to help people fulfil their potential.

For those fortunate enough to be involved in coaching, there are few greater rewards and pleasures than seeing other human beings grow and change as people and take greater control over their own life. That change process is a critical aspect of what the psychological dimension to coaching is all about.

The essence of coaching

If you pick up a collection of coaching books you'll find a wide range of perspectives on the purpose, function and methods of coaching. With so many angles and viewpoints it can be difficult to find precisely what the coaching *thing* is and how it differs from other similar activities such as consultancy, training, and counselling. Yet there are important differences and one of the best ways to find them is to explore the basic principles of coaching. This is where you will find its essence.

Sound coaching principles

Working to a set of sound coaching principles greatly enhances the likelihood of successful outcomes. It also acts as a guiding influence to keep you on the coaching side of the tracks. A number of the principles I set out here apply to all types of coaching whereas the systems perspective and business focus are more specific to executive coaching:

1 From tell to ask.
2 Performance and potential.
3 Awareness and responsibility.
4 Building self-belief.
5 Business focus.
6 Systems perspective.
7 Coaching as a mindset.

1 From tell to ask

The first and probably most important is that you are there to assist the learning, development and change of the client through facilitated learning and not by *tell*. This most profound of notions is at the heart of good coaching and defines its essence. Learning through the coaching method is an inside-out process, not an outside-in one. It assumes that people often know more than they think they know and are capable, with help, of understanding and resolving issues and moving forward in their lives through reflective learning.

This adult learning principle has become better understood but it is still counter-cultural in many business, sporting and educational contexts where *tell* still rules. Even those who have started to see the benefits of the coaching approach – a greater capacity to think for oneself, heightened self- and social awareness, a greater sense of personal responsibility, better self-management and enhanced self-belief regularly fall back on the instructional, advice-giving, expert mode. It's a hard habit to break.

2 Performance and potential

The second fundamental principle of coaching is that we need to focus not only on current performance but also on potential. This means changing the lens from how individuals are performing now to how they may perform in the future if they are able to tap into their inner resources and capabilities.

Typically, people do not know what they are capable of doing. They may intuitively sense that there is more and have a strong desire to find out, but may not know how. They need someone to help them unlock it, and that is the job of the coach.

Aside from the skills and experience a coach brings to this situation there is another aspect, which we should never underestimate, and that is the power of believing in someone. In the early stages of coaching clients may not have a strong sense of themselves. It can therefore be invaluable for them to experience someone else, whom they respect, and to believe in them. It can keep the candle burning.

3 Awareness and responsibility

The third coaching principle is the importance of awareness and responsibility in coaching. Indeed it is the common ground between most, if not all, coaching authors and is captured in the proposition that awareness is the starting point for growth and change. As people become more aware of their assumptions, belief systems, attitudes and behavioural patterns they move into a position of choice – to stay with them or to change. The responsibility for this choice is with them.

Awareness of issues may be no guarantee of change but it is certainly an essential precursor. We are unlikely to change something if we are currently unaware of it. Awareness is our route into ourselves, others and the relationships between us. It is the foundation of our capacity to self-manage and self-regulate. This means that the coach needs to appreciate the primary place of awareness-raising in the coaching process and how to facilitate it.

The issue of responsibility is just as central to coaching and indeed to any change process. The coach may facilitate the heightening of a client's awareness through running a 360-degree feedback exercise providing an ocean of rich data but if the individual doesn't own any of it, then the prospect of learning and change is low.

Taking responsibility for one's choices and actions is like getting into the driving seat of one's life. It is about taking charge of our lives and accepting the consequences of our decisions and actions. For some people this can be a difficult process, especially where damaging experiences have left their mark. In these circumstances the coach has an important job to do – to help people to believe and trust in themselves and others. This may take the coach to the boundary between coaching and therapy but it can be an essential journey to take. Coaches will not always have the luxury of working with highly motivated, uncomplicated individuals who already take full responsibility for their lives. Indeed one of the most rewarding aspects of the coaching role can be when someone who has been struggling to occupy that driving seat finally feels able to do so and takes off down the road.

4 Building self-belief

The fourth principle is linked with the second for, although it's important for the coach to believe in the potential of the client, it is even more important that the individual begins to recognise that their success is down to their own efforts. This is the process of building self-belief – the growing confidence that derives from accumulating successes and achievements.

Bandura (1997) is best known for his significant contribution to our understanding of what self-belief is and how we develop it. He uses a different term, self-efficacy, to describe 'people's beliefs about their capabilities to produce designated levels of performance'. He argues that our level of self-efficacy determines how we feel, think, motivate ourselves and behave. Those with high self-efficacy approach difficult tasks as 'challenges to be mastered rather than as threats to be avoided'. They set themselves challenging goals and sustain a strong commitment to them even in the face of setbacks. Bandura considers that this outlook produces personal accomplishments and reduces stress and vulnerability to depression.

Framed in this way it is easy to see why coaching is about the development of this outlook. Bandura gives academic credibility to what Henry Ford said many years earlier: 'Whether you think you can or cannot, you are right.' Coaching seeks to enhance the belief that *one can*.

Building self-belief is a core aspect of what coaching is about and is strongly associated with personal growth and behavioural change. Successful coaching leaves people feeling stronger in themselves as if their inner core has grown.

This, together with the previous three principles, constitute the core principles of all coaching and are what makes it different from consultancy, training, and counselling – despite the similarities with all these learning processes. For executive coaching, however, there are two additional principles and guidelines to keep in mind – a business focus and a systems perspective.

5 Business focus

Executive coaching is primarily concerned with the development of the executive in the context of organisational needs. It can be tempting for the coach to temporarily forget the organisation and instead work exclusively from the perspective of the executive as client. Some coaches don't have a great deal of experience of corporate life and others may hold little sympathy for the ways in which some companies treat their people. In these cases the organisation's agenda can get jettisoned. This, however, will carry a cost. The client may feel better, even vindicated, by the coaching experience but the person paying the bill will often be left frustrated and disappointed. It has to be acknowledged that the balance is not always easy to find but experienced coaches tend to find their own ways of satisfying both agendas and it is an essential part of the apprenticeship of novice coaches.

Keeping the business focus will also be critical to the development of coaching as an emerging profession. If organisational clients don't see sufficient tangible benefits from coaching then it will become sidelined and perceived as just another organisational fad that failed to deliver.

6 Systems perspective

One of the most important business competencies for executive coaches is sufficient knowledge and awareness of organisational dynamics and systems issues. O'Neill (2000) stresses a systems approach to executive coaching when she makes the following important points:

- *When we focus too narrowly on the client alone – her personal challenges, goals and inner obstacles – you can miss the whole grand 'ecosystem' in which she functions.*
- *It is essential to pay attention to the system as it generates forces that have an enormous effect on your client's success.*

This systems perspective is most clearly in evidence when individuals try to change their behaviour in a team culture that neither understands nor supports that change. Sometimes colleagues actively seek to keep the person acting in old ways because there is some perceived benefit to the group. An example of this would be the team joker who wants to be taken more seriously but his colleagues are happier with the status quo and persuade him to stay as he is. The problem, from his perspective, is that he is constantly overlooked for promotion despite having career aspirations because senior management are not convinced that he can command respect. Or the over-controlling, somewhat aggressive manager who wants to change some of these behaviours but his boss is worried that he will lose his edge.

This might suggest that the system tends to subvert individual change and this is not necessarily the case. There are many occasions when the system actually has a positive reinforcing effect, which gives encouragement to the individual to stay with the programme. Coaches need to facilitate this scenario whenever they can by involving the system from the outset and educating colleagues of the client that they have an important role in the success of the coaching effort.

Where behavioural change does take place it's also crucial to recognise the effects on other people in the system. Executives tend to be very aware of how difficult it is to sustain behaviour change and to greater or lesser degrees possess a systems perspective themselves.

7 From coaching as a tool to coaching as a mindset

The final principle is a more general one and applies to all types of coaching.

Coaching opportunities occur every day and we miss many of them. One of the reasons for this is that coaching is often equated to coaching *sessions*. In other words it is framed as an activity. So, I want to challenge you to notice coaching opportunities beyond the formal arrangements you already have in place. These are the short conversations in the corridor, in the car travelling to a meeting, on the phone, over a cup of coffee, on the move. These may last 20 minutes and they may take no more then two.

Whether coaching is primarily conducted in a formal or *ad hoc* fashion, the bigger picture is that its contribution goes far beyond its application as a management tool. Coaching's true power is that it can literally be a way of thinking, even a way of life. It can be the principle upon which we interact with others in every aspect of our lives.

PART 1
A framework for effective coaching

1   Good coaching process

Introduction

Good coaching process follows a similar sequencing to the classic organisation development methodology of engagement and contracting, data collection and feedback, action planning, implementation and follow-through and evaluation, which either leads to termination or a recontracting for further work. What follows is my adaptation of that methodology for the purpose of executive coaching.

The stages of a good coaching process are:

1   Engagement and contracting.
2   Assessment and feedback.
3   Creating the coaching agenda.
4   Structuring the coaching intervention.
5   Delivering the coaching.
6   Review and evaluation.

Stage 1: Engagement and contracting

Engagement

Although you may think of contracting as the first phase of the coaching process there is typically a detailed preliminary exercise undertaken before this stage is ever reached. Purchasers or sponsors of coaching services nowadays go through increasingly rigorous arrangements to establish the quality and credibility of the coach and the fit between the coach, the client and the organisation. They also give the client an opportunity to meet more than one prospective coach to get a feel for personal chemistry.

In this early contact between the prospective coach and client both parties are asking similar questions such as: 'can I work with you?' and 'how do I feel around you?' Clients may want to gauge whether they feel safe with the coach and whether the coach will be too challenging or not challenging enough. They certainly want to know whether the coach seems to understand them and grasp their dilemmas, concerns and challenges. Results-focused executives will be keen to establish whether the coach is experienced, practical and able to communicate in everyday business language and not management development or psychological jargon.

As a coach you will assess the readiness and motivation of the client, give information about the coaching process and begin to clarify the goals and likely focus of the coaching. Some coaches approach this engagement process in a fairly practical, hands-off way. Others see it as the opportunity to demonstrate what it will be like to work together. In this case, the session becomes more than an informational exchange and engages in real work. The advantage of this is that you get to see the reaction of the client to your approach. The client gets a much better sense of what will be in store. Sometimes coaches are reluctant to use the opening engagement session in this way because they are working without being paid for it. They may also be concerned that the contract to do real work has not yet been established. For these reasons coaches typically err on the informational side but give a taster of their style and preferred ways of working.

The issue of chemistry is a complex one. For some prospective clients the overriding consideration is whether they feel comfortable or not with you. Others may recognise that some degree of discomfort might not be a bad thing – it may suggest a more productive working relationship. Which way clients go on this issue is often determined by their present level of vulnerability or a historic issue around feeling safe enough.

For you as the coach, the chemistry issue is also relevant. A positive liking and an immediate empathy for the client will always feel better and give you that reassuring sense of looking forward to the work. However, experienced practitioners recognise that, on occasions, the most unlikely and least promising of starts can turn into some of our best and most satisfying assignments. Your challenge as a coach is to find out what it is that makes this client difficult for you. That said, there may be occasions when you simply don't wish to take a client on. There may be little motivation or even downright hostility from the prospective client at the idea of being coached. You may have a strong clash of values or an intense negative reaction to some individuals and choose not to work with them.

Contracting

The purpose of contracting is twofold: firstly, to facilitate more productive outcomes and, secondly, to reduce the likelihood of misunderstandings and failed expectations in the future. You do this by establishing both the personal and organisational objectives for the coaching and by clarifying everyone's roles and responsibilities in the process. Certainly, anyone who supervises coaches will tell you that many of the problems further down the line have their origins in the contracting stage. The coach may not have been clear enough about expectations and outcomes, the confidentiality agreement or some aspect of the business relationship.

You should therefore undertake this phase with care and consideration to a range of issues:

1   Is it a two or three party contract?
2   What are the desired outcomes of coaching?
3   What will be expected of each party (coach, client and sponsor)?
4   What is the confidentiality agreement?
5   What are the reporting arrangements?
6   What will be the scope and method of assessment?
7   How will the coaching intervention be structured?
8   Where will the coaching take place, how often and what levels and availability of support is being offered?
9   How will the coaching process be reviewed and evaluated?
10 What are the business arrangements – fees, cancellation terms and invoicing procedures?

The nature of the contracting process will depend on whether it is a two- or three-party arrangement. Sometimes a chief executive or managing director will want to keep the arrangement two way. He may not want the board chairman involved or may feel that he wouldn't be interested anyway. When coaching is used to address the executive's own agenda it can be entirely proper for the contract to be two-way. However, you will want to satisfy yourself that not having a third-party organisational sponsor is appropriate.

Another reason why some contracts are two way is that the business leader or owner is paying for the coaching herself and it is a private arrangement. She may want to look at her career or wider life options and prefer to keep this as a personally sponsored activity in which she is not beholden to the organisation to link her own coaching agenda to business objectives.

Most organisational coaching, however, is a three-party contractual relationship. Often referred to as the triangular contract it involves an organisational sponsor as well as the coach and client. The sponsor may be the client's line manager or the HR director or manager. Usually you or they will set up a series of meetings to bring all three parties together with the purpose of clarifying the objectives for the coaching, which will typically focus around strategy, performance, development, behavioural change or a mixture of all of these.

In an ideal world the list of items presented as the coaching agenda will be both clear and achievable. There will be a shared perception of the issues by both the client and the sponsor as well as a high level of commitment to the coaching process. And fortunately this does happen on some occasions.

Inevitably, however, it is not always as straightforward as that. Clients may see things very differently from the sponsor yet withhold their perspective in order to be seen to be complying. The sponsor's coaching agenda may be vague, insubstantial or inappropriate. As the coach you may be placed in the position of saying the difficult things to the client which the organisation has backed off from saying. This is most definitely a situation to avoid and your task in these circumstances might be to challenge the line manager or HR sponsor to be far more candid with the client.

In larger scale coaching initiatives senior executives often have to come up with desired coaching outcomes for several of their direct reports and due to busy schedules, throw a few thoughts together in a rushed and unconsidered manner. Worst of all is the situation where the organisation wants to exit the individual and the coaching process is set up as a protective measure to demonstrate that all attempts have been made to support the individual first. In these circumstances you might be told that things have reached a critical point and this assignment is the final opportunity for the client to save his job. Experienced coaches will be wary of these situations and stay clear of coaching assignments where the individual has already been written off.

Confidentiality

The contracting process should certainly address the issue of confidentiality. In the two-party contract this is fairly straightforward. Unless you learn of some criminal activity or the client presents as a danger to himself or others then you observe the confidentiality agreement you have made. If you are in professional supervision, and this is now seen as essential to good practice, then you need to disclose to your client that you discuss your work with a supervisor who is also bound by a confidentiality protocol.

In the triangular contract, confidentiality can be more complicated. The organisation will want to know whether and to what extent the coaching objectives have been achieved. Feedback into the system is part of the process. The issue is more about what can be said and to whom. The standard guideline is that personal content is kept confidential and progress towards the coaching goals is the appropriate focus for review and evaluation. Clients and sponsors alike tend to be content with this arrangement and you won't go far wrong if you stick to this. The danger is when you get coopted into the system and align consciously or unconsciously with senior figures. This is a common scenario. It can be very tempting for coaches to experience themselves as having the ear of the powerful person in charge. Clients can be very aware of this and remain watchful as to whether anything they have revealed to you comes back round to them through their boss. If this happens, trust will inevitably be affected.

Expectations of the coaching process should be articulated at the contracting stage. The sponsor and client will have theirs but so will you as the coach, and these need to be stated also. Some coaches demand that clients undertake homework in between sessions. Others have very strong views about punctuality and cancellation of sessions. Some coaches only undertake to be available for scheduled sessions and crises; others offer more flexible contact arrangements. Behavioural coaches often view the coaching process as taking longer than some other types of coaching activity and may seek to contract for at least a full year if not longer.

Most coaches, sponsors and clients like to see some or all of this enshrined in a written contracting document signed by all parties. Producing this document gives a formality to the process that suits many sponsors and clients. However, it doesn't suit all. Some organisations and coaches are less happy to be tied down and prefer a more open-ended, emergent process with less formality.

The final aspect of the contracting process is your responsibility as coach to provide the organisation with a copy of the code of ethics to which you subscribe. Coaching does not yet have one established overall professional body but there are a number of professional associations such as the International Coach Federation (ICF), the European Mentoring and Coaching Council (EMCC), the Association for Coaching (AC) and the Association for Professional Coaches and Supervisors (APECS), all of whom publish ethical codes and require their members to ensure their clients are aware of them.

Stage 2: Assessment and feedback

Assessment

Many executive coaches see assessment as a crucial part of the coaching process. It can provide information on a client's personality, thinking styles, emotional intelligence, leadership, learning preferences as well as identify strengths and areas of development.

There are many different ways to approach assessment, which include structured assessment or development centres, the use of instruments such as MBTI (Myers Briggs Type Indicator), 16 PF (Sixteen Personality Factors), FIRO-B (Fundamental Interpersonal Relationships Orientation – Behaviour), emotional intelligence profiling, 360-degree feedback, one-to-one or group interviews and taking a developmental history.

Many assessment instruments can only be administered by trained psychologists. Peltier (2001), observes that psychological testing and assessment is 'one essential area where psychologists have a clear edge over all other kinds of consultants' and argues that assessment represents psychology's 'historic core competency'.

Psychometrics says Wasylyshyn (2003) 'cannot be underestimated as an efficient way to surface relevant information and insights' and Kiel et al. (1996) make the point that executives 'trust data' and therefore come to trust the executive coaching process when data are provided.

Experienced coaches tend to have their own favoured methods of assessment. Coaching psychologists often hold strong affinities to particular psychometrics but others believe that 360-degree feedback is a more useful method of data collection as it brings together a wider range of perspectives and adds that vital dimension of impact on others.

In addition to psychometrics and 360-degree feedback questionnaires there are several other means of assessment such as observing the executive in the workplace and interviewing colleagues close to the client – peers, direct reports and the manager. Taking a detailed life history can also be helpful as it produces the bigger picture of someone's life and may reveal important themes and events that later help the coach to contextualise emerging issues.

The breadth and depth of the assessment stage should be tailored to the situation. It is not always necessary or appropriate to undertake a full-scale process. Coaching assignments sometimes follow on from internally run assessment processes or a few months on from a 360-degree feedback exercise. It can therefore be uneconomic in time, effort and budget to repeat such a process. It often makes more sense for you, as the coach, to read all the data available and perhaps supplement it with some one-to-one conversations with the client's colleagues.

In her review of the use of psychometrics in coaching, Rogers (2004) raises an important point when she says 'the most important question to ask is why you are using a psychometric questionnaire at all'. She notes that new coaches are often attracted to these tools and techniques out of anxiety. The prepared report arising from a proprietary process can provide you with a sense of being on safe ground. Rogers rightly warns that coaches can be tempted to use questionnaires indiscriminately whether or not the client really needs them. My own experience as a coach trainer confirms this and I regularly observe huddles of course members intensely quizzing another delegate as to the latest psychometric or EI instrument that he or she has just been accredited to deliver. What often lies behind this anxiety is a fear of whether turning up and asking 'how do you want to use this session?' will be enough. Will the client bring any significant issues, will there be enough to talk about, and will I, as coach, be good enough?

This is not to devalue the place of assessment tools as they can be enormously helpful in raising a client's awareness but you do need to be clear why you're using them, be properly trained, and not become over-reliant on them. They are a means to an end, not an end in themselves.

Rogers makes another interesting point when she notes that they can also disturb the balance of power in the coaching relationship. Instead of the client determining the agenda the coach is back in the expert role and we know how quickly that can result in the client reverting to passive rather than proactive learner. Although Kiel et al.'s (1996) point that executives trust data is probably true, we should not forget that professionals also hold on to expertise – it acts as a comfort blanket.

Feedback

The assessment process can take many forms but the most important aspect of it has to be the delivery of the data. Accreditation courses to train coaches and consultants in the use of psychometrics involve the coach experiencing the process herself. However many coaches have not personally experienced a 360-degree feedback exercise. The idea of having several colleagues and possibly customers and even family members giving detailed feedback about us would be enough to throw most people into a blind panic. Yet this is what we, as coaches, are regularly asking others to do. Most managers try to take a positive view and bravely say that they are bound to learn something useful about themselves. Some dread it and don't believe they should have to subject themselves to it. Either way it should never be taken lightly or without sufficient preparation.

Nor, when we take someone through a battery of tests, should we forget that the data can reveal a great many soul-searching questions for the client. This may be fascinating to some and torment to others. All of this depends to a large extent on four things: the client's personality, the method of delivery of the report, the skills of the coach, and the degree of positives versus negatives in the data. Someone who finds negative feedback very difficult to hear will require highly skilled delivery. Every experienced coach who uses 360-degree feedback knows the feeling of looking at a report in advance and thinking 'oh dear, this one is going to be hard'! These can be the heart-sink moments of coaching. They can also be some of your most important development opportunities. They take you out of your comfort zone and demand that you work at your best.

The capacity to work with feedback is a fundamental aspect of coachability and so the formal feedback session provides some clear indicators as to future coaching potential. To ensure the session or sessions are productive it's important to bear in mind some practical as well as emotional guidelines. One of the most important is to leave sufficient time to do justice to the volume, breadth and depth of the material. Often coaches don't schedule in enough time or they allow their clients to shave time off allocated diary time. A useful guideline is to schedule 2 to 3 hours for a 360-degree feedback report session.

It may be self-evident but it's important to stress that you should not simply send reports to recipients to open, read and digest on their own.

This kind of practice does happen and can do more harm than good. It also undermines the credibility of the assessment/feedback process. There can be severely negative messages coming through processes of this kind for some clients and they require proper, skilled support to deal with them.

Stage 3: Creating the coaching agenda

Sometimes coaches are far too vague in the early stages of the coaching process and don't pay sufficient attention to the creation of a clear coaching agenda. This can later lead to a nagging feeling of dissatisfaction in the coach and sometimes an early termination of the coaching by the client. However, if the assessment stage is undertaken properly then this should provide more than enough data to feed into the coaching agenda.

Another source of input comes from the sponsor (in the triangular contract). The client's manager or HR director will be the third party in the coaching relationship and she will typically have identified a number of desired outcomes from the coaching process. These should have been explicitly discussed in the contracting meeting. Then there is the client himself who may or may not have a list of issues he wishes to bring to coaching. Some clients know exactly what they want to use their coaching for; others benefit from a more structured and facilitated approach to creating the coaching agenda. Here are three actual coaching agendas formed out of the processes described above.

First, Anthony's coaching agenda:

- Create a more performance and customer-focused culture.
- Improve the performance of my top team.
- Become more effective at managing upwards.
- Decide what to do about an underperforming director.
- Improve my self management.
- Learn how to be more influential.
- Become more strategically focused.
- Create a better work/life balance.
- Think about how to position myself for the next job.

Second, Susan's coaching agenda:

- Reinvigorate enthusiasm – 'I've lost a little spark'.
- Reevaluate my management style.
- Manage my time more effectively.
- Coach and develop my people more.
- Address some personal development issues: 'I'm told that I'm intimidating and prickly'.

- Think about succession planning.
- Let go more and trust my team.
- 'Think about where I'm going and whether to stay in corporate life or make a radical change of lifestyle'.

George's coaching agenda was:

- Think through some issues in the work situation.
- 'It can be a little lonely at times and I need more support for myself.'
- Challenge myself more.
- Improve self-regulation.
- Improve the quality of my relationship with my boss.
- Ensure that I feel included.
- More effectively manage my emotional responses.

The range of themes covered here includes:

- strategic management
- organisational politics
- managing upwards
- team performance
- emotional intelligence (self- and relationship management)
- behavioural change
- personal support
- leadership development
- thinking time on problem issues
- inclusion
- personal challenge
- work/life balance
- career progression
- meaning making

It is commonplace to arrive at such broad-based coaching agendas and this list underlines the need for the executive coach to possess a wide range of business, coaching and psychological proficiencies.

Stage 4: Structuring the coaching intervention

You may have favourite ways of structuring a package of coaching, such as six sessions of 2 hours spread out over 6 to 12 months but it is important to hold the principle of flexibility in mind. One of the hallmarks of coaching is that it is tailored to meet the needs of the individual and the organisation. Therefore you need to look at each situation with fresh eyes and be careful of falling into too rigid or formulaic ways of structuring coaching packages.

Sometimes the situation calls for an urgent response such as when an executive is experiencing a crisis. You may need to offer more support for a while before easing off and resuming your normal schedule of sessions.

It can sometimes be helpful to involve more than one coach in the delivery of the coaching and there may also be real benefits in shadowing your client in his work environment. Some clients value the opportunity to contact their coach between sessions by email or phone – some never do. The key point is to look at every coaching situation freshly. Take into account the client's needs and design the intervention for that person.

Remember also that the venue can be a critical factor. A manager is not going to open up about a serious issue if they are having their coaching session in a hotel lobby. Or, if they do, they may later become self-conscious and embarrassed by the lack of privacy. You need to ensure that the physical space provides a proper environment in which deeper more intensive work can take place if necessary.

Coaching usually takes place over several months and you should be aware that different kinds of challenges will lie ahead. The one certainty about the human condition is that our lives constantly change. We may think at the beginning of the process that we are clear about the coaching agenda only to find, further down the line, that some significantly more pressing issues come to the foreground. If you work flexibly, you can bend with the situation and address the important needs emerging at the time.

Stage 5: Delivery of the coaching

We have now arrived at what all the preceding parts are there to inform and support – the coaching delivery. Actually, this is not strictly true because coaching will have been happening all the way through in different guises. Nevertheless, there is a time when all the diagnostics and preparations are complete and the series of coaching sessions starts. This is when the importance of good coaching method comes into play. Here are some guidelines, tips and reminders about what constitutes good coaching.

Being fully present

First and foremost you need to be fully present. Coaching is a dialogue not an interview. That means really getting engaged and making genuine contact. To do this, it can be helpful to prepare yourself mentally and emotionally before sessions to minimise distraction and be ready to focus in the moment. Just as sportsmen and women warm up to get focused and ready for performance, and their coaches loosen up with them, so executive coaches need to find their ways of switching into coaching mode. Some coaches take time to read notes from previous sessions. Others ensure that they have some quiet time to get focused.

I emphasise this because I firmly believe that things happen when we are in contact – contact with ourselves, our client and the relationship between us. Conversely little happens when we are not in contact. So here is the first challenge – to be fully present. If you are, then one thing's for certain: you'll soon know whether your client is. If he isn't, due to distractions and a busy mind, then the session may remain at a relatively superficial level and neither of you will feel very satisfied at the end of it. If there are several sessions of this nature then there is a distinct possibility that the busy executive will drift away. Sessions may get cancelled and your attempts to get the schedule back on track may seem unduly difficult. For these reasons it essential that you confront, perhaps gently through humour, the issue of whether clients are finding it possible to really bring themselves into the coaching space.

When fully present, both coach and client can decide how best to focus and use the session. Early sessions often address the prioritised and targeted issues arising from the coaching agenda. It may be obvious to both sides where best to start and, as a general rule, a momentum begins to develop. New sessions pick up from where the last one left off and agreed actions are reviewed for key learning points.

Both parties will share a desire to maintain momentum and feel that progress is being made. When it isn't, you as the coach need to have the courage to voice your concern and be prepared to acknowledge if you feel that you might have a part in it. This may take you into a review of the quality and depth of the coaching relationship to see whether any blocks have developed.

As trust builds and rapport grows stronger, the coaching process develops a life of its own and often becomes highly enjoyable and rewarding for both people. Clients look forward to their sessions despite a slight trepidation at again placing themselves in a vulnerable position. They feel 'held' by the coaching and a sense of psychological security grows.

To ensure that clients feel able to tackle their most pressing issues it is essential to balance support and challenge within the coaching dialogue. Too much support over time and too little challenge can leave a client under-stimulated and even bored. Too much challenge without sufficient support can produce stress and an unsafe environment for learning. Some coaches struggle to find the balance. They either have difficulty conveying empathy and warmth or lack the capacity to confront and rock the boat. This may be a block for some coaches and require supervision and personal development to understand it more clearly.

A key to maintaining momentum lies in the coach's ability to get to the core issues. This is where a greater level of psychological competence can help because many complex coaching issues invariably have an inner dimension to them as well as an outer one. Executive clients typically have a high expectation that their coach will be able to get to the heart of a matter and this is one of the key competencies of an effective executive coach.

Many coaches work on the assumption that they will act as the only coach for their client throughout the entire period of coaching delivery. For some clients this is very important, especially where trust and confidence in the coach has been hard won and is not to be risked lightly. However, there can be value in the client being exposed to different influences and I sometimes suggest that one or two sessions take place with a different member of my coaching team. Typically the reason for doing this is to provide clients with an opportunity to work with someone who may just bring a coaching presence, through their own unique skill sets and life experience, which adds value for the client. No coach can be all things to all people. Sometimes the client may need a stronger psychological focus or a more strategic one. And sometimes I simply follow a hunch.

If you are thinking of suggesting that your client works for a little while with another coach then you need to ensure proper preparation takes place. It does have its dangers. The client may feel passed on or even rejected or abandoned. It can only be done if you have built a solid coaching relationship and it will be inappropriate with some clients. There is a risk for you too. What happens if the client likes the other coach more or rates his or her skills more highly? New coaches should probably take their time before considering this intervention and make a point of consulting their coaching supervisor before committing to anything. However, in my experience, it can add to the quality of the coaching experience for the client and should be borne in mind as a coaching delivery option.

Practical arrangements

The locations where most executive coaching is delivered are the coach's consulting rooms, the client's office or training suite, and hotel conference facilities. Some coaches favour telephone and electronic coaching and many use these methods to supplement their face-to-face work. Little research yet exists to tell us how effective coaching that is not face-to-face can be compared with contact sessions but there is little doubt that many executive coaches feel the need to offer both. There is an obvious logic to this. Clients may have just left their last coaching session when a highly significant new issue emerges that they would like to run past their coach. If the next session is scheduled for four weeks time then the whole episode may pass by. The client wants help now. For this reason alone it is advisable to have an open door for more immediate needs to be dealt with. The coach may fear that this could be abused by clients – I have to say that this has not been my experience. Executives are often overly self-contained and require many offers before taking up extra assistance.

Extras

A very important gesture, usually well received by busy executives, is the spontaneous reach out. This is where the coach thinks of something that might just be useful to a client and acts on that thought. It might be an article in a newspaper or journal, a card to wish the person luck before a promotion board, or a short email to stay in touch. Some clients appreciate the gift of a book and despite the apparent lack of interest shown by many executives in management literature there are those who genuinely value recommended readings or CDs.

Availability is also a critical issue for the coach. The more successful you become the cleverer you need to be in managing your time so that you remain available to your clients. Purchasers of coaching services are often concerned that the executive coach may be very busy and ask just how much time the coach really has to devote to executives.

One final point about the delivery of coaching, which finds its way into a number of coaching texts, is the notion that the coach should care as much for the person as the results. This first appeared in Gallwey's writings on coaching. Caring does not appear on too many coaching competency lists but it is fundamental to any helping activity. The kinds of people drawn to practising as coaches will tend to have a strongly developed caring side to their natures. The message here is not to be afraid to express it.

Stage 6: Review and evaluation

Review of outcomes and return on investment are two of the hottest topics in coaching today. Business has now had a good look at coaching and wants to know what it is getting for its money and how success is to be measured.

It is, however, one of the topics that make many coaches feel least comfortable. Not that we disagree with the principle of evaluation; rather, we still don't have standard methods that both produce the desired result and are relatively pain-free for organisations that commission coaching.

Some coaches favour the 360-degree feedback method at the beginning and the end of the coaching process with a half-way stage meeting to review objectives. This has logic to it although it can be unworkable when the coaching project involves large numbers of people. Most busy managers will not thank you for asking them to fill in several lengthy and time-consuming 360-degree feedback questionnaires twice within the space of a year or less.

An answer to this can be to use customised, paired-down versions that specifically focus on the desired coaching outcomes.

A simpler process of evaluation, which many coaches adopt, is to use the original list of coaching objectives identified at the contracting stage and schedule a review meeting at the half-way stage and another at the end of the coaching delivery. These meetings typically include the sponsor, the coach and the client. The process involves each party sharing his or her perspective about how much (or little) progress has been made as a result of the coaching. Differences of view can be expressed, but the norm is that a consensus emerges. If coaching has worked well then everyone knows and acknowledges the fact and if it hasn't it's just as obvious.

You may wish to conduct a more extensive process of evaluation involving a series of interviews with the client, her manager, peers, direct reports and any other significant parties. This enables you to produce a detailed report bringing together several perspectives. If the organisation is prepared to invest the required time and budget to undertake this work then it can be an excellent method of coaching evaluation and is to be recommended.

All this relies on having clear coaching goals in the first place and this is not always the case. Sometimes coaches go forward from the contracting stage knowing that the goals are not explicit, but they tolerate the situation – only to regret it later at the evaluation stage. This is another reason why it is best to be strong and clear at the beginning. If you can't easily articulate the purpose of the coaching immediately after the contracting then you may have a problem waiting for you further down the line. Check that you really understand the coaching agenda and also whether it's something that can realistically be delivered. Then, when it comes to review and evaluation time you have a platform to return to.

As for the bigger picture of how successful coaching is proving to be as an organisational intervention, I would caution you not to be too extravagant in your claims. There are a small number of studies that have produced the sorts of results which make for good reading. Unsurprisingly these get quoted a great deal, especially on coaching Web sites, and as marketing soundbites on business development documents, but it is still early days in terms of research into coaching outcomes. There is comparatively little in the way of reliable, comprehensive research into organisational coaching outcomes.

Summary

In this chapter I have set out a six-stage coaching process adapted from the classic organisation development model. You may be left wondering whether the coaching process always needs to follow this sequence. My view is that it most often does. When we fail to contract clearly enough we invariably store up problems for the future. When we don't undertake a sufficiently robust diagnostic process we can miss some fundamentally important aspects of the client's outer and inner worlds. When we don't pay enough attention to the creation of an agreed coaching agenda we can find that the coaching soon runs out of steam. And, unless we review and evaluate the coaching process then how can we know whether it has worked?

The main variables where discretion and tailoring applies will be the extent and nature of the assessment and evaluation processes, the number of client sessions offered and how they are delivered. The general running order however will usually be much the same.

2 Critical success factors in executive coaching

Introduction

The coaching field is still some way from establishing the critical success factors of executive coaching. Advocates of particular models and approaches may believe that they already possess the answer but, whatever your starting position, there can be little doubt that the three elements of the coaching dynamic – the coach, the client and the relationship between – must feature strongly and significantly.

The coach's competence and professionalism

It stands to reason that the skills and experience of the coach must be critical factors in effective coaching. But what is it that makes coaches excellent, good enough or downright incompetent? This is a question being asked by a range of people involved in the coaching business. Purchasers of coaching services need to know what 'excellent' looks like in order to make sound decisions about procurement. Clients naturally want to know whether their coach is up to scratch. Coach training providers need to address the question in order to make informed judgements about how to train and develop coaches. Specialist coaching companies offering executive coaching in the marketplace need to take a view in order to recruit wisely.

Having worked with a great many coaches over the years, and trained many more, two aspects stand out. The first is the overall competencies of the coach and the second is professionalism. I single this out because it is so fundamental to good practice.

I'll begin by looking at the issue of coaching competencies, something that has been occupying the minds of many in the coaching field for some years. However, there is another question that needs to be addressed alongside it: competency for what type and level of coaching? The competencies of line-management coaching may have certain commonalities with those of the professional executive coach but there will be some differences and clearly one would expect a very different level of competence. Similarly, the career coach, the domain-specific coach or occupational psychologists primarily involved with assessment/feedback coaching will possess some specialist competencies in-depth but will not necessarily have the full range expected of a generic executive coach.

The competencies offered here are specifically geared to executive coaches and are based around five higher level categories: *business, coaching, psychological, interpersonal skills/relationship management and professional practice.*

Business competencies include corporate awareness and 'savvy', understanding of organisational dynamics, leadership, strategy, culture, and politics along with the general ability to move in corporate circles with a fair degree of comfort and surefootedness. Without these things, the executive coach may not gain credibility and acceptance. This is applicable to both internal and external coaches.

Coaching competencies are a combination of skills, process, method, mindset and clarity about the role. Some believe that the coach with strong coaching competencies doesn't really need some of the other competency areas, particularly business and psychology, because a good coach can coach anyone whatever their background and occupation. This is an appealing notion with some truth in it. However, a closer examination of the role of the executive coach in particular, will reveal coaching agendas and contexts that require the coach to possess a broader knowledge base and skill set.

Psychological competencies for coaching are grounded in psychological mindedness – the capacity to reflect on the causes and meanings behind one's own and other people's behaviour, thoughts and feelings. Awareness – both self awareness and awareness of others – is fundamental to this. Coaching assignments often have a behavioural dimension to them and require the coach to understand how change takes place (and why it often doesn't) as well as possessing behavioural coaching skills. The importance of the assessment stage of the coaching process also suggests the need for training in assessment methods and techniques. For the executive coach, there can be advantages in having a counselling or psychotherapeutic training in order to diagnose more complex psychological issues in the corporate world as well as coaching executives through critical phases of their lives.

Interpersonal and relationship management competencies are a combination of relationship building and relationship-development skills. These include communication skills, the capacity to establish and maintain rapport and trust, to demonstrate a non-judgemental stance, and to express warmth, tact and diplomacy. The capacity to manage the triangular contracting arrangement is also a feature of this competency category.

Professional practice competencies include the following: honouring confidentiality agreements, acting with integrity and working ethically and to a recognised code of ethics. It means to deliver on promises and consistently to demonstrate the highest standards of professionalism. It also requires of you, as the coach, that you take responsibility for addressing your learning and development needs through continuing professional development (CPD) and a commitment to coaching supervision.

Relevance of professional background

The degree to which coaches possess this wide range of competencies will depend on their professional background, training and experience. In my experience most coaches, novice and more experienced, have development needs in at least one of these category areas.

To a large extent clients understand who their coaches are and what they bring from their previous work and life experience. Some niche coaching consultancies build up their businesses by appointing 'names' from the corporate or sporting worlds and trade off their reputations and contacts. Some of the corporate ex-directors and CEOs-turned-coaches bring enormous organisational experience and may well have strong interpersonal and relationship management skills but often lack appreciation of the difference between coaching and consultancy and generally possess little or no psychological training. They can therefore slip quickly into the role of strategic advice-giver from the 'been there, done that' mindset. Similarly, ex-sportsmen and women may be excellent coaches but can be reliant on extrapolating the ingredients of success from sport and can be oversimplistic in their suggestions about how these can provide answers for the business world.

Human resources directors, management trainers and organisation development specialists often have a broader spread of competencies but typically lack any substantive psychological training and background. Psychologists, psychotherapists and counsellors will be stronger in the psychological domain and may possess good interpersonal and relationship management skills but often lack corporate knowledge and experience.

No one starts off a career as an executive coach so it is inevitable that those who come into this emerging profession will bring some, although not all, of the five higher-level category areas. This is just how it is and it doesn't need to be perceived as a negative. The issue is more about finding appropriate training and development to address the gaps – a critical challenge for many executive coaches.

The professionalism of the coach

Coaches are often privy to highly sensitive, delicate, personal and business information. You may know that one of your clients is about to be sacked before he does. A client may reveal that she is struggling with whether to whistle-blow on her boss about financial irregularities. The CEO may tell you that the company is about to be taken over – news that will not be communicated to the staff for several days. It is therefore incumbent on you to observe the highest standards of professional practice in terms of confidentiality and discretion. It is paramount that executives have full confidence in their coaches to keep things safe and secure.

Many, although not all, coaches work to a code of ethics available and reputable coach training providers include professional issues as part of their syllabi. Those coaches who come from professions such as psychotherapy, counselling and clinical psychology will have been inducted into long established and very clear professional guidelines.

Concerns nevertheless exist around this whole area of sound professional practice. There are many entrants to the coaching field who are keen to offer themselves as professional coaches but possess little relevant training and experience and have probably never considered professional practice issues. They don't work to a code of ethics, may have unclear professional boundaries and often haven't heard of professional supervision or do not understand its purpose.

This is important for several reasons. The ones that most concern experienced coaches are to do with professional standards and the danger that poor practice on the part of some may reflect badly on others and upon a newly emerging profession seeking to establish itself as reputable and credible. Coach training providers who promise that they can turn out professional coaches in 2- to 5-day courses only add to this concern.

A further worry is that well-meaning but poorly trained and inexperienced coaches may do more harm than good. They may form inappropriate relationships with their clients, which lack professionalism. Examples of this regularly surface, for example, where coaching relationships suddenly turn into intimate relationships.

Purchasers of coaching services want to be reassured that the coaches they seek to hire are professionally competent. Those on the receiving end of coaching need to be able to trust their coach's ability and integrity. One of the most important aspects of executive coaching is the capability to maintain confidentiality and act appropriately amidst complex organisational dynamics and politics. Sound professional boundary management is critical.

But professionalism should not only be seen as a set of 'do nots'. There is wisdom contained in codes of ethics and guidelines on good practice, often hard-won through mistakes of the past. There is also pride and enjoyment to be derived from knowing that you are operating at the highest levels of professional practice. It inspires confidence in you and in your clients. They can trust that you are a safe pair of hands.

The coaching relationship

The quality of the coaching relationship is regarded by many coaches not just as *a* critical success factor but *the* critical success factor in successful coaching outcomes. The coach creates a safe enough space for the executive to take the risks necessary to learn, develop and change.

Characteristics of a successful coaching relationship

Kilburg (1997) outlines the following characteristics of a successful coaching relationship:

- Predictability and reliability.
- The 'hygiene' factors of time, place and confidentiality; fees and cancellation procedures are properly set out from the beginning as well as the coach's expectations about homework, etc.
- The coach displays respect, consideration and understanding for the complexities of the client's experience.
- The coach demonstrates empathy for the client.
- The coach interacts in an authentic and genuine fashion and provides an experience of non-possessive regard.

Kilburg also lists a number of behaviours that the coach needs to display toward the client, which include: respect for the client as a person; consideration and understanding for the complexities of the client's life and his/her inner world; courtesy; accurate empathy; and tact.

Practitioners familiar with the philosophy of client-centred counselling will recognise similarities with Kilburg's list. This shouldn't be surprising given the immense impact of the client-centred approach pioneered by Carl Rogers.

The influence of client-centred thinking

Rogers (1961) proposed that there are a number of 'core conditions' that determine the quality of the therapeutic relationship and help create an environment for growth and development. They are: unconditional positive regard and acceptance, accurate empathy, and congruence/genuineness. Unconditional regard means communicating a deep and genuine caring, which is non-judgemental. Congruence means that you act in accord with your values and belief system, seeking to be real and genuine in your interactions with other people. Accurate empathy is about understanding the other person's world from their subjective reality.

It is now half a century since Rogers coined his 'necessary and sufficient' conditions of beneficial outcomes and an extensive body of research has confirmed his views. Nevertheless his core conditions are a challenge for many coaches. In coach training programmes I regularly hear delegates admit that they have difficulty in taking a non-judgemental stance. Many also have problems expressing empathy. They think that if they understand the client's thoughts and feelings then that is enough.

Empathy, however, is more than whether you think you understand the other person's world. It is whether you communicate that empathy in a meaningful way. It is about conveying and expressing something – a thoughtful, sensitive comment or a caring gesture.

Establishing rapport in the coaching relationship

The coaching relationship is dynamic. It grows, develops and changes over time. And sometimes it doesn't. There may be occasions when it hardly gets off the blocks. The great value of the Rogerian framework is that it can provide you with some of the reasons why that elusive good contact hasn't materialised.

Most coaches can recall clients who they haven't warmed to at first meeting. That feeling may be reciprocal. The good news is that this often changes. Because of the dynamic nature of relationships it is always conceivable that a good connection can emerge from cool beginnings. If you, as the coach, are able to facilitate the core conditions then the client may feel more prepared to reveal their vulnerabilities and take the risk of being open to you and the coaching process. This in turn may produce a different reaction in you.

On occasions, this may require you to look harder in the mirror and ask yourself: have I really been fully present with this client? Have I hidden myself yet expected my client to do the opposite? If the answers to these questions are that you have stayed too protective of yourself then you have a new question to ask – 'am I ready to take more risks with this client and really be there for him/her?'

Relationship skills may be a development issue

For some executive clients the very issue they most need to address is their capacity to form effective relationships. Goleman's (1996) emotional intelligence framework identifies four main elements: self awareness, social awareness, emotional self-management and relationship skills. Executive coaching often addresses development needs in one of those areas and it is common to coach senior managers on relationship skills. The issue may surface through a 360-degree feedback process, performance appraisal, team development session or assessment centre. It can also be brought to attention through more formal mechanisms such as grievance allegations.

The coaching relationship can be the experimenting ground for the client to gain feedback on how he is coming across. Colleagues at work may be reluctant to give straight, tough feedback but you, as the coach, are expected to. The coaching relationship can provide the vehicle for here-and-now feedback based on how you experience your client's styles of interacting, communicating and connecting.

Some clients want this delivered in a tactful, sensitive and caring manner; others insist that you pull no punches and tells it as it is. One of the constant challenges for coaches is to appreciate their clients, and the culture in which they work, so as to tailor their style and approach accordingly.

Recognising the client's strengths and achievements

By and large those who come for coaching are relatively or even exceptionally successful people. They possess considerable strengths no matter what context you happen to be meeting them in. It is therefore important to affirm both the achievements and the person. Affirmation from a peer, someone trusted and valued, is a very significant thing in anyone's life. Most people get so little of it.

You may be the only person with whom the client has an equal professional relationship. He knows that coaching will inevitably involve looking at developmental issues and what he needs to improve and change. Yet he also needs to hear that you can see what he is doing well and that there is another more positive story – one of accomplishment.

Very often it's precisely this affirmation that encourages your client to continue with his journey of self development, especially when the going is tough. When you really recognise your client you add an enormous deposit to the relationship bank.

The issue of trust

Any discussion of the coaching relationship would be incomplete without acknowledging the importance of trust. Trust enables clients to feel safe enough to say whatever they need to and reflect on mistakes and short-comings. This takes us straight back to Rogers, because if the coach is not accepting of the client and worst still, conveys a judgemental stance, then the client will certainly back off. He will also be far less likely to go there again in the future.

Trust has several dimensions but two are especially important to coaches. The first is to do with integrity and the second concerns competence. Integrity is about maintaining confidentiality and acting with tact, sensitivity and honesty. One careless comment or act of gossip can completely undermine trust and potentially wreck the coaching relationship.

Trust in the person is vital but so is trust from the client's side in the coach's competence. Competence problems arise when the client experiences the coach as suspect in approach, judgement or behaviour. Despite the fact that most coaches know that their job is to facilitate rather than tell, some can be prone to drift into giving advice. The client who is looking for answers from the coach may initially appreciate any pearls of wisdom emanating from you but will soon become wary if the quality of that advice proves to be dubious. More experienced clients who understand that coaching is essentially a facilitative process may be left wondering whether you really understand your role. Another version of this is when clients feel they have been taken into deep emotional terrain by a coach who lacks the skills and understanding to operate as a proper guide and safety net. This can lead to a deep sense of anxiety in the client.

Competence, then, is as important as integrity in building and maintaining trust in the coaching relationship. One of the ways it is transmitted is when you, as the coach, clearly know your own strengths and limitations and act within them. This is an important aspect of professionalism.

The coaching relationship is not just a critical success factor in coaching but may be the most important one. If so, this has obvious implications for coach training. Programmes that are model based and technique based may need to include a greater emphasis on the coaching relationship and how to equip coaches with a higher level of relationship-building skills. It may also imply a stronger focus on how to both challenge and support more effectively.

One of the great values of having a coach can be the experience of someone really being there for you and encouraging you to believe in yourself and achieve your goals. When clients look back, years later, on their earlier experiences of being coached, more often than not, they bring the coach as a person to mind, not the tools or psychological frameworks that the coach used. Those individuals who have never been coached in a formal sense may have some similarly important figure in their life who performed the same function. We tend to have a warm feeling when we recall these people. It might be a parent, a relative or a teacher from school. Those people, coaches or not, leave a deep and lasting impression.

Client factors

It would be tempting to think that if coaches are reasonably competent and professional in their approach, work to sound coaching principles and with a good process, can connect with people and form strong helping relationships, then positive coaching outcomes will surely follow. After all coaching works, doesn't it?

There is, however, another important factor in the equation and it may be the most important – the client. Up to now little attention has been given to the issue of whom coaching works best with, and whether everyone is potentially a suitable candidate for coaching. The result is that coaching has been offered far too indiscriminately in many organisations with greater consideration being given to whether the coach is the right person than whether the potential client is right for coaching. This has inevitably led to some poor results from significant investments of money and has left questions in some people's minds about the value and benefits of coaching.

One of the most pressing research needs at this time is for evidence that guides both coaching purchasers and practitioners towards better coaching outcomes and the selection of who should be offered coaching and who should not will inevitably be a key aspect of this. The danger of simply throwing coaching at entire layers of management is obvious. It will work well with some but not all and some may then become disillusioned and talk coaching down.

Some coaches don't help matters in their overzealous claims about what coaching can achieve. The emerging coaching profession has to look at itself here for colluding with a degree of hyping up – something that has created its own problems. What is needed now is a more considered look at how coaching works, what competencies and qualities an effective coach requires and with whom it works best.

The coachability framework in Table 2.1 may provide a basis for thinking about this latter point – which managers and executives are most and least likely to benefit from coaching. My hope is that this will assist both coaches and coaching purchasers to make more informed decisions about where to concentrate effort. The framework may also be of value to coaching supervisors.

Interpreting the coachability framework

This framework is based around five levels of coachability from excellent through good and average to poor – the fifth level suggests, for example, that coaching is an inappropriate form of intervention at this time where severe psychological problems exist. The top column includes such issues as

Table 2.1. Coachability levels

Severe psychological problems	Inter-personal problems	Perceptions of others	Threat of career derailment	Performance issues	Motivation for coaching	Coachability level
Absent	Absent/low	Excellent/good	Absent	Absent	High	**Excellent**
Absent	Absent/low	Excellent/good	Absent/low	Absent/low	Medium/high	**Good**
Absent	Low/medium	Medium	Low/medium	Low/medium	Medium	**Average**
Absent	Medium/high	Medium/poor	Medium/high	Medium/high	Variable: low–high	**Poor**
High	High	Poor	High	High	Variable: low–high	**Inappropriate to intervene right now**

performance, degree of interpersonal problems, threat of career derailment, and motivation for coaching, which are critical factors in determining the likelihood of positive coaching outcomes. They do nevertheless require further clarification.

Level 1: Excellent coachability

I want to start this by asking you a question. Take a moment to think through your coaching experience and look for strong, clear examples of people you have coached who you would unambiguously place in the *excellent coachability* category. I would suggest there may be very few.

This is because *excellent coachability* is not so much demarcated by the absence of negatives but by the presence of strong positive factors. These include: a powerful commitment to improve continuously, a hunger to learn, and a desire to be the best one can be. People in this group set high standards for themselves. They rarely want or need them to be set by others, and their benchmark is always excellence. They understand the need to learn from experience, look upon failures and setbacks as part of the learning process, and tend to bounce back quickly when things don't go according to plan. They also appreciate their responsibilities as role models and act with a high level of awareness of what leadership entails. People in this group also share the need for new challenges and have a strong commitment to their own personal growth and development and that of other people.

They bring all of this and more to the coaching arena. Their motivation is high, they are ready to work, and will turn every piece of gold they acquire in the coaching session into tangible actions that benefit not just themselves but also those they work with and serve.

All of this may sound too good to be true and might suggest that coaching must be an absolute breeze with this type of person. Yet there is another aspect to it. The very same high demands they place on themselves also tend to be transferred onto you as the coach. They want the best and they want results. This can scare some coaches, who get caught up in their own internal dialogues of: 'am I a good enough coach for this person?' or 'will this client rate me?' This self-interference can then adversely affect the coach's own performance through anxiety or trying too hard.

Working with people of this kind can also be exciting and stimulating. The bar is high for both parties and there is often an edge to the work. One of the things they often want is challenging, insightful feedback and if they get enough of it they are delighted. Typically, they don't get the quality of feedback they are looking for in their everyday lives.

As you've been reading this you may have thought of professional sportsmen and women – athletes, golfers, rugby, soccer or cricket players and the like. I say this because most successful competitors are great examples of the qualities described above. Certainly in my own experience of working in professional football as well as business there are many football coaches who demonstrate this eagerness to learn and improve. They are always looking out for that little nugget of gold which will give them an edge.

In the business context there are also managers and executives, as well as more junior staff, who fit these criteria and are therefore prime candidates for coaching. However, the danger can be that coaching is not offered to this high-performing group but instead to those with performance problems. People in this first category can get missed out on the pretext that they don't need it as they are already doing so well. The point that is sometimes missed is that coaching works best with precisely those people who are already performing at a high level yet still want to set their sights higher.

Level 2: Good coachability

When executive coaching is offered to senior management groups and entire layers of upper management there will be many who fall into this second category. People don't reach senior positions unless they have a strong results focus and responsibility drive. They then take that into their coaching. In other words they recognise that the organisation is investing in them, take it seriously and try to get what they can from the process.

Managers with a good level of coachability are likely to bring very few negatives such as performance problems or interpersonal relationship issues to the coaching process. They present as interested and open to whatever they can get from it. Unlike the first group they may not always have that extra desire and hunger to improve or seek out feedback so avidly. They may be in a comfort zone, unclear about what they want from their coaching. The thinking goes something like this: 'I haven't got any serious problems so I'm not sure what to work on in my coaching sessions.'

In this situation you may need to pay greater attention to helping your client to understand the wider potential of coaching and to think beyond problems. It can be helpful for clients, especially those new to coaching, to be taken through an exercise that reveals the breadth of possible coaching agendas. Working new clients through a list of this kind can help them form a robust coaching agenda at the beginning of the process.

Motivation for coaching can vary in this group, usually between medium and high. One of the common features of the *excellent coachability* group is their exceptionally high level of motivation but this will not always be the case at level two. This can present a problem if you have an expectation of a higher level of engagement. You may then unwittingly project that onto your clients in the form of disappointment, frustration or irritation for not using the coaching opportunity productively enough. Patience and perseverance on the part of the coach is often the answer to this as people in this group typically warm to the process once they begin to see clear benefits. Commitment levels can rise during the course of the coaching.

Returning to the question I posed earlier about how many clients you've worked with who genuinely fit the *excellent coachability* criteria, I suspect now that you have considered this second level, quite a few of your clients more closely fit this description. Exceedingly high levels of motivation and desire to improve are probably rarer in organisational life than we first think.

Level 3: Average coachability

Few people would be happy to be described as average unless, of course, they have been struggling to climb out of a poor performance category. The processes of 360-degree feedback can reveal to managers that others do not perceive them as strongly as they assess themselves. Their self-perception can be at the good or very good levels, but they might find that others consider them nearer to adequate or average.

Most companies have been raising their expectations of performance for some time now and what used to be regarded as acceptable has changed, leaving some people stranded or fighting for their jobs. Those in level 3 therefore differ from level 2 in one very significant sense – they are potential career derailers. That brings huge implications for their coaching.

Managers and executives in this category of coachability often find their way into coaching as a result of an assessment process, or as a consequence of a performance appraisal. They can be strong in the technical aspects of their jobs and there may be few if any performance issues in that department.

Their developmental issues are more likely to show up in their team leadership, interpersonal relationships and emotional intelligence. If they have undertaken a 360-degree feedback exercise there is usually a mixed picture of strengths and areas of development. There may also be a few unpleasant surprises.

Following a process of this kind there will be an expectation that the individual turns this new self-knowledge into improved performance and coaching is sometimes offered as a support structure for achieving this. In these circumstances coaches will typically look out for signs that the client appreciates the need for change and is showing an earnest desire to address developmental issues. The catalyst for this can be a threat to the person's job security. Although this is clearly a difficult starting point for coaching it can have a galvanising effect as well as providing a clear set of coaching goals. If the individual remains closed to the feedback then coaching can be hard work because the client is not just resisting the feedback and those who have provided it but is also resisting you.

Motivation, then, can vary enormously in this third level of coachability and will be a significant factor in the success or failure of the process. It should also be noted that motivation is contagious and therefore the effect of the coach will itself be a potential influencer.

When the client demonstrates a real commitment to change, you, as the coach, will usually feel moved to do your very best for the client. When you meet resistance, especially over a prolonged period, your own commitment and motivation can be affected. When this happens it can be helpful to bring such issues to your supervision and explore how your clients' sense of hopelessness is impacting on you.

Working with people in this category can be the hardest of all. At levels 1 and 2 you can expect good to high levels of motivation and commitment from your clients; at level 3 it may go either way. For this reason it's important both for the organisation and you as the coach to be clear about what is expected from the coaching and whether the client is really bought into it.

Level 4: Poor coachability

Poor coachability denotes a situation where performance problems exist and the perception of the client by significant others such as bosses, peers and direct reports is laden with negatives. This immediately suggests a poor prognosis yet in some ways it is easier to work with people in this category than the preceding one. In this scenario everyone usually knows where they stand. It is coaching to save the client's job. A word of warning however – it's absolutely essential that you satisfy yourself that the client has not already been written off by their organisation otherwise the coaching will be a charade and leave both you and your client with strong negative feelings.

Unfortunately it is not always possible to get a clear picture of how the organisation perceives the situation and you may be unable to clarify its intentions. And even when you think you know, the situation can change part way through the coaching engagement and leave the original brief in tatters. Coaching in this context is therefore fraught with problems but it also contains opportunities to make a real difference at a time of crisis in a person's life when his or her job is at risk.

The behaviours and attitudes that have brought the individual into trouble are often replayed in the coaching relationship. Some of these are likely to be emotional intelligence issues where the client displays a low level of self- and social awareness. You may experience the client as talking at you rather than to you and feel like an object rather than subject. The client may go into long, rambling and off-the-point stories, which leave you bored and frustrated. Deflection and lack of contact may characterise the interaction. When you try to focus things or offer feedback it may appear to bounce off and simply produce another long-winded story.

Though this type of situation will inevitably be challenging it may still be possible to work towards good outcomes. The more troubling scenario is when the client also has serious performance issues regarding the technical side of their job. Coaching is unlikely to contribute a great deal here and so it is very important at the outset to check whether these exist and, if so, how much they are playing a part in the total picture.

Tackling behavioural and emotional intelligence agendas invariably requires a degree of candour not always necessary with other groups and not always easy to express for the coach. Some coaches are more comfortable in the evocative, supportive mode. They may be wary of conflict and have a strong need to be liked. This may prove to be an obstacle when working with people in trouble. You may need to deliver a level of robust feedback that challenges the client's deep-rooted, defensive routines. Otherwise there is the danger that there will be no impact and, consequently, no change.

If a breakthrough is achieved it usually involves a risk either on your part or from the client. He may share some deep worries about what the loss of his job would really mean to his family and to his own self-esteem. Powerful feelings may be expressed, which might test your capacity to support someone with strong emotional needs.

Some coaches avoid working with people in this category for understandable reasons. There is a lot at stake, client motivation may be dubious, and the company may not even be telling the entire truth about its intentions. On top of that the client might be difficult to reach and appear virtually impenetrable. These are all good reasons to work exclusively with clients from the excellent, good and average coachability categories. But there is another perspective to be considered.

Executive and career derailment is a feature of our time. The statistics show that it is increasing. It's a financially expensive problem to companies and an alarming, often devastating blow to individuals. If coaching can help some people avoid it then surely it's worth trying. This may be the occasion when it works.

Level 5: Inappropriate intervention right now

The key differentiators in this category are to do with psychological and medical problems. Where these exist and have been identified, coaching is often an inappropriate intervention. These situations are far from commonplace but they do exist in organisational life. Examples include depression, severe anxiety and addiction. There are also instances of executives suffering from schizophrenia and personality disorders.

If the condition is recognised then the possibility of treatment presents itself and in most cases this will be performed by clinicians from the medical and mental health services. Typically the manager will be away from work for a period of time followed by a planned return to work. In many cases this produces the desired result and the manager resumes his career. Sometimes, however, it breaks down and the individual leaves the organisation on the grounds of ill health. In this scenario the primary helping partners are the professional medical and psychological services and, at the organisational end, the person's manager, peers and HR department.

The above scenario assumes that the condition is identified, diagnosed and treated. Sadly this is not always the case and every organisation has its number of psychologically complex individuals, some of whom may be in senior positions. Colleagues might suspect they know the problem but don't know what to do about it. Conversely, and this will often be the case with people with personality problems, they experience all kinds of difficulties with the person but don't really understand what they're dealing with. Situations can drag on for months and even years with devastating effects. The condition just never gets diagnosed.

On some occasions the HR department contacts an external coach, perhaps someone known to have psychological or therapeutic training, hoping at least to gain some further understanding of what they are dealing with. Or they may refer the individual to an internal company doctor who then sets up a referral with a psychiatrist. Typically however these scenarios run and run. The confusion in the system is compounded by a fear of litigation if the company fails to cover itself properly.

But there is another reason why some of these situations are not addressed sooner and it's to do with the bottom line. Some of these executives may be perceived as delivering strong financial results and their companies don't want to lose them. They can be highly aware of the cost in terms of damage to close colleagues but make a cost-benefit analysis and decide they'll live with that in order to secure the financial benefits.

As a coach you need to be aware of this fifth category. Organisations in their desperation to get help, or to cover their backs, will sometimes look to coaching as a way forward. Typically this intervention is unlikely to work and, worse still, carries with it a degree of professional risk. If you think that you might be working with someone with a more complex psychological makeup then it is important to take this to your supervisor to gain another perspective and support.

Other client factors

The question of which factors are the most significant in producing successful outcomes has been studied in depth within the counselling and therapy field over many years. Given the infancy of executive coaching there is no comparable body of research to draw on yet, although this is likely to be addressed in time. Until then it makes sense to consider some of the key learning arising from the numerous studies that have sought to identify the *common factors* that contribute to change. An important summary of this research by Assay and Lambert, in Hubble, Duncan and Miller (1999), identified four major factors in therapeutic success: the client; the relationship; hope/expectancy; and models/techniques. They attributed 40 per cent of success to client factors, 30 per cent to the relationship and 15 per cent each to hope/expectancy and models/techniques. In other words this research suggests that it is clients themselves and the circumstances of their life situation that account for the most important element of the change process. So what are those life situation factors that play such an important role in change?

They consist of the client's own inner strengths and external supportive elements in their environment, such as friendships and family, membership of a close networking group, religious affiliation, hobbies and leisure activities.

The inner factors – self-belief, motivation, persistence and sense of personal responsibility – are also key ingredients and if they are present there is a greater likelihood of successful outcomes.

This can be seen as a very positive way of looking at personal change. Prochaska et al (1994), whose studies on change processes have informed behavioural coaching models asserts 'it can be argued that all change is self-change, and that therapy is simply professionally coached self-change.'

The *common factors* research may contain some useful messages for coaching. The client's inner strengths have already been identified in the coachability discussion as vital to success – particularly their motivation to engage in learning and change. It may be useful for coaches to remember how important the client's external environment can be. If clients are trying to change deep-rooted ways of thinking and longstanding patterns of behaviour it should be obvious to us that they will stand a much better chance of succeeding if they have effective supports in their personal life.

Finally, we should not miss the crucial point that ultimately the coach's job is to help clients to self-coach. From this perspective, the coaching relationship can be seen as a fundamental bridge that leads eventually to more effective self-support.

PART 2

What coaches deal with – common themes and issues

3 Common themes and issues brought to coaching

Coaches are often unclear about what count as valid coaching themes and issues. There is little reference in coaching literature to the sorts of topics and themes brought to executive coaching. It is therefore timely to take a closer look at just what coaching deals with. The discussion of these matters will reveal some of the stronger psychological dimensions to coaching issues. This list has been compiled with the coach in mind but should also be of value to clients who are not entirely clear how best to use their coaching. You may wish to discuss this range of coaching themes in the early stages with your clients.

1   Skills and performance
- Learn a new skill/ grow a capability
- Solve a problem.
- Make an important business decision.
- Adapt management style or make behavioural changes.
- Improve personal performance.

2   Personal development
- Obtain closure around some unfinished business in the work situation – for example, a conflictual working relationship.
- Develop emotional intelligence.
- Develop deeper self-belief and confidence.

3   Leadership
- Prepare for a future leadership role.
- Become a more effective leader now.
- Develop influencing skills.
- Become more strategic.
- Create a high-performance team and organisation.

4   Meaning making
- Find greater meaning, satisfaction and balance in your life and work.
- Discover what you really want from your life.
- Make a major life change.

4 Skills and performance coaching

Learn a new skill

Skills coaching is a form of on-the-job learning. Very often conducted by the line manager, some companies embarking on the coaching culture journey have also employed team coaches whose primary role is to work alongside their team members to assist with skill development. This is increasingly common in call centre environments. The purpose of skills coaching is to reinforce induction and training-course learning. It is particularly relevant in the early stages when an individual is getting to grips with the requirements of a new job. Typically, it's during the first 6 months of a new role when it becomes clearer what the job really requires and development needs begin to surface. However, skills coaching can also be important further down the road when individuals feel that they have plateaued or need to move to a high level of competence.

Skills coaching is appropriate for people of all levels from the very first career position right the way to top leadership roles. The specific skills may vary but the needs exist just the same. One of the major obstacles to those needs being met is the cultural phenomenon common in many organisations that senior managers shouldn't need development at this level. After all, if individuals are deemed suitable for an executive position and are being paid a large salary then they should be capable of just getting on with it.

At executive and senior management levels the skills issues that most regularly present at coaching are to do with how individuals present themselves. They are about interpersonal, presentational, negotiating and influencing skills. In essence they are about how the person comes across and the impact it leaves.

Grow a capability

Growing a capability is a slightly different challenge. It can focus around the need to multitask and deliver large volumes of work accurately and speedily. More and more is expected of today's managers and staff and the capability to deliver against tight deadlines is a given. This requires the ability and desire to learn – and learn fast. Indeed this particular capability is now a key proficiency in business life. Those who can learn quickly are highly sought-after individuals. Helping people grow their internal engine to cope with increasing pace and complexity is a key role for coaches and potentially one of coaching's most relevant contributions.

This type of coaching can take the coach into directive mode at times: something that won't trouble some coaches but may be uncomfortable for others. On-the-job coaches, for example, often mix advice, information and guidance with feedback.

Solve a problem

> The coaching process allowed me to think through and solve or take to the next stages some taxing management and personal problems. These range from re-organising the department to dealing with staffing issues. The key to it is that the coaching session forces you to put time aside to consider them. These issues are often easier to avoid in the short-term but build up to bite you later. (Gerry)

One of the great misconceptions that new coaches pick up is that coaching is not about problem solving. Try telling that to your clients and they will probably nod in agreement and then proceed to tell you their problem anyway. Of course coaching is about problem solving. Indeed, it's the help which clients experience in sorting out their problems that they typically value most about their coaching. Whilst people want new insights about themselves and their situations they also want practical ways forward.

The process of solving problems involves gaining great clarity about the issues and these can be both internal (inner) as well as external (outer). The issue, for instance, might be a difficult relationship with a colleague or boss. The external dimension may be to do with a conversation that still needs to occur to resolve some previous conflict. The internal may be the fear of addressing that conflict and where the conversation might go. For example, your client may be apprehensive about upsetting someone else or placing herself in a position of vulnerability.

The inner and outer game

In our training of coaches we often refer people to Timothy Gallwey's (1974, 2000) inner game coaching theory. His influential insights about how our outer game is impacted by our inner game are fundamental to understanding performance, be it in a sporting or business context.

The inner game is our psychological world where our potential, our hopes, aspirations and desires sit alongside our fears, doubts, self-limiting beliefs and assumptions. Many of our trainee coaches begin with a strong tendency to look for the solution to the client's problem in the external reality – the outer game. They eagerly race towards a practical set of actions often before fully understanding the complexities of the issue in the first place. This is hardly surprising given that the action focus is such a prized and valued activity in organisational life. The action plan is often the all-important outcome from any business meeting. However, the flaw in this approach soon becomes evident when solutions drawn from hasty, superficial dialogue fail to meet the requirements of the situation.

When we slow down and examine issues more thoroughly, becoming more aware of the process we are really dealing with, a new factor often emerges into the equation – ourselves. In other words we begin to recognise that the problem we have previously seen as an external issue – outer game – also has an internal – inner game – element to it. We start to see how we are or have contributed to the problem and how we may need to change our part in the script. Or we may realise that the very way in which we perceive the issue is the main problem. We may be making assumptions that don't stand up when properly examined or we may be failing to acknowledge some of our own behaviours as part of the problem. Maybe we have a strong need to be right and a belief that we usually are, or an inflexible belief system about how people and the world should be. When others don't conform to this, we see them as wrong and resort to blaming rather than examine ourselves. Of course, there are some problems that contain a relatively minor inner element to them. However, clients tend to solve these on their own.

The important message here is that significant performance issues, the things that most trouble and confound people tend to have an inner as well as outer dimension and this is one of the primary reasons coaches need to enhance their psychological understandings and competence. From this perspective the process of coaching people on solving problems needs to operate on both the outer and inner levels.

Make an important business decision

Clients bring their tough decisions to coaching. Should I take the risk to expand? Do I need to let some of my people go? Do I stay with the team as it is or do I take the difficult decision to replace someone I have serious doubts about? How do I increase revenue? Where can I reduce business costs? How do I change the culture of the company? How do we help our people keep up with the rate of change in the company?

These are just a small selection of business questions brought by clients to their coaching. They know that they have critical business decisions to make but haven't yet been able to make them. They want a sounding-board to weigh up the issues involved and move closer to decision-making and action. What they may not recognise at the outset is that their dilemmas have an inner as well as outer game element to them. If they do realise this, they may feel stuck about how to move forward.

Case illustration

Despite steady growth in this small company, Signpost Marketing, the directors had been reluctant to grow their cost base and had held off making the decision to take on more staff. Instead they continued to stretch themselves and their small business team and rely on freelancers to outsource extra work. This is a fairly typical scenario in any small business and has some virtue in it while also containing the seeds of a number of problems. The company directors decided to use some experienced facilitators to help them think through the issues, identify and evaluate options, and arrive at a preferred way forward. The facilitators were excellent at the outer game level. They quickly got the scent of the business problem and encouraged the group to brainstorm a range of future scenarios. Having produced several pages of flipchart material the facilitators finally confronted the directors with the inevitable question, 'Well, what are you going to do then?' The question was delivered in a friendly, well-intentioned manner. It seemed obvious to them that after such a good process the answer would be there. It wasn't. Instead the directors both confessed to still not knowing what action to pursue. Later, when they revealed their inner game they said that they had felt panic and a little stupid because they have should known. They felt they were not being good clients and had disappointed the facilitators who themselves later admitted to feeling frustrated with them. The rational process should have worked but in this case it was not enough.

Further review revealed that the outer game focus had been helpful but the inner game had barely been addressed. When asked what their inner game had been both directors acknowledged the depth of their doubts, uncertainties and fears. They accepted that some of these were probably irrational and exaggerated but they were present nevertheless.

What they wanted was to be able to surface them, take a look at them and understand them better. Perhaps then they would have chosen to let some of them go, or at least would have realised that they weren't yet ready to. Either way they would have moved on a little. Importantly they both wanted their inner world to be acknowledged and affirmed, however rational or not it sounded.

The facilitation did produce something of value. Intellectually they felt clearer in their minds about the issues involved and the options available. But they still felt blocked about taking the critical decisions.

Implications

There are several implications arising from this case illustration. The first is that difficult decisions are often made after a great deal of deliberation and going around the same issues time and again. Secondly, the use of an external facilitator or coach can be a useful sounding board to achieve greater clarity. Thirdly, an exclusively outer game focus, which is the norm in most business consultations, often fails to address key blockages to action and progress.

The proposition here is to learn how to coach more competently and appropriately at both the outer and inner levels in order to facilitate what Gallwey refers to as mobility. Mobility is that sense of energy and forward momentum that comes with clarity of thought and purpose. It often emerges when that feeling of stuckness, confusion and uncertainty melts away to be replaced by new awareness and insight.

The facilitators in our story would say that they were aware that inner issues were present. They picked up some of the signs and signals. Like many consultants, facilitators and coaches they were happier to stay at the outer game and were unsure about where to take the inner game.

Learning how to do this is one of the most common development needs for coaches today. But let's be clear that, although this story illustrates some psychological dimensions to coaching issues, this is not therapy, nor is it in-depth psychological work. What we are talking about here is giving people an opportunity to express some of their fears about change, their self-doubts, and those familiar concerns and ambivalences that prevent them making decisions and taking steps into the unknown.

Adapting management style or making behavioural changes

Sooner or later most managers and executives become aware of the predominant aspects of their management style. Some come to it on their own; others have it brought to their attention through appraisal processes, assessment centres, 360-degree feedback, coaching and team development activities or formal HR processes.

They may be perceived as hard driving, overcontrolling or departmentally rather than company focused. Bosses and colleagues may be constantly asking them to slow up, let go a little, become more of a team player and see the bigger picture. On other hand they may be seen as too laid back, conflict-averse and reluctant to deal with performance issues. The message these managers may be receiving will be more about urgency and getting to grips with underperformers.

Each and every style has its benefits and drawbacks. Naturally, managers have mixed views and feelings about being asked to change their style. Some cling to the belief that their success is based around their predominant style and if they were to change it then their effectiveness would be diminished. In any case they can't see why they need to change and are dubious about whether people ever really change anyway.

On the other hand some managers enthusiastically grasp the feedback and present as eager to learn anything they can that might improve their performance and themselves as individuals. They just want to know how.

Whether your client is in the first or second group the initial work tends to be about clarifying and understanding what is being said. Clients inevitably put their own interpretation on the feedback they receive and sometimes the key messages are so different from their own view of themselves that it simply doesn't make sense to them. Getting it in perspective and scaling it to its correct size is often the first task.

Widening the repertoire

It can be helpful to frame the work as widening the managers' repertoires rather than a fundamental change of style. That repertoire includes both their behaviours and strategies for dealing with the array of issues facing them. Some of the difficulties managers and executives get themselves into can be a direct result of having too narrow and rigid a repertoire of responses and strategies. When something or someone challenges them they quickly run out of listening, patience, tolerance and the ability to see it from the other person's point of view. Their ability to self-regulate and self-manage reaches its limits. At its worst the next step can be an angry outburst although many people never get that far. Instead they may snipe, become sarcastic or quietly withdraw.

Some managers may feel that they are being asked for too much – to change fundamentally who and how they are. Except in rare circumstances it is better to avoid framing behavioural change in such extreme terms. This will almost certainly produce resistance, fear or apprehension. Instead, the notion of widening one's repertoire may be more acceptable, achievable and productive in the longer term.

One of the most common changes requested of managers is to get their heads up and see their people as well as the task. This doesn't come easily to some managers, especially those who derive their personal satisfaction and sense of value from the technical side of their job. What may seem obvious to the HR manager or coach – that the individual would get the job done even better by attending to both the task and the people – may be anything but obvious to this manager who hears the message as just another thing to fit into his busy day.

Companies who have chosen to take the coaching culture journey struggle with this challenge of getting their most task-focused managers to see the value and benefits of developing their staff. One of the most productive ways to achieve this is for the manager to receive good coaching himself and, through this experience, begin to see the payoff of doing it himself with his own team.

Improving personal performance

Many organisations now expect their managers and staff to be far more conscious of their work performance and to want to improve it. Most of my coaching is performed in the business context but I also coach in professional sport. Going from one world to the other is always an interesting experience and I would strongly recommend executive coaches to seek opportunities out to work in sport too. Both worlds have much to offer each other. Many sporting organisations could benefit from some of the professional leadership and sound management practices of corporate life. Equally, business executives and managers could gain from the performance mindset and understandings about preparation, anxiety management, focus, and desire to win from competitive sport.

When working with sports coaches I often encounter a keen desire to glean any piece of information, technique, method or idea that might make a difference to performance. Encouragingly, they are often inner as well as outer game focused and committed to improving their own performance as much as that of the team to which they belong.

There are increasing examples of this in corporate life as people become more and more aware that standards are continually rising and that they need to stretch themselves more than ever before. Some have not yet caught on fully to this and may be in danger of getting left behind.

This is the context for coaching for improved performance and it is likely to become even more critical as the pace of change and the upward spiralling of expectations continues to gather pace. In today's fastest moving companies senior executives are acutely aware of a major new problem facing them – how to help their people develop as quickly as the company is developing.

Career-threatening performance issues

Clearly there can be a host of performance problems brought to coaching and it is not my intention here to produce a comprehensive list. Rather I want to focus on a small number of critical performance themes. Research conducted for the Lore Institute by Spencer Singer (2001) has reinforced findings from the Centre for Creative Leadership in the US suggesting that if these issues are not satisfactorily resolved then the individual is in danger of career derailment. The four problem areas are:

- Difficulties adapting to change.
- Failure to build and lead a team.
- Emotional intelligence.
- Failure to meet business objectives.

Difficulties adapting to change

Organisational restructures, a change in market conditions, or simply a change of boss are all significant change issues which can present difficulties for a manager. If that individual is not seen to be making the correct adjustment, or is not doing it quickly enough, then questions can arise as to whether he has what it takes to operate in the new situation.

When someone is thrown into an unfamiliar role they may overrely on a previous style or revert to behaviours that don't fit the new scenario. They may need to learn some new ways of acting. Most managers recognise this and make the necessary adjustments by learning new skills, increasing their technical knowledge and widening their behavioural repertoire. Coaching can be a useful vehicle for this, providing some of the essential feedback mechanisms to alert individuals about whether they are on course and moving fast enough.

External changes in the business environment can also produce high-level challenges for managers and executives. Changes in the economic climate quickly impinge on most business sectors and produce testing conditions for senior people. An executive may have produced excellent results for many years on the back of favourable economic conditions only to find that a much tighter climate is resulting in a serious downturn in sales in his area. Colleagues will then be watching to see whether he can adjust his steps and find new answers.

Internally, the company may be going through a cultural shift perhaps brought about by a new chief executive or as a response to the external market. The new values, norms and expectations may present problems for some people. In these situations it is common for the individual to be offered coaching either as a positively intentioned form of assistance to get up to speed or as a safeguard for the company in the event that the person is later exited and takes legal action.

But one of the most common change issues to affect managers is simply a change of boss. It is common for managers to find that their boss changes every few months and the expectation is that the subordinate does most of the adapting. The unspoken rule runs something like this: learn what the new boss likes and doesn't like, make their priorities yours, show loyalty and don't publicly step out of line. Most senior managers don't need this spelling out and make a special point of managing their relationship with the boss to their mutual advantage. When they have those inevitable differences of opinion they handle them with care and skill.

Managing upwards

Getting to grips with the boss relationship, or managing upwards as it is often called, is a critical factor in how a manager is perceived. Some managers have problems in this area for a number of reasons: difficulty reading the boss, not finding ways to respond effectively or a downright refusal to make the necessary adaptations in the first place. The goal of coaching in these circumstances is to improve the boss-subordinate relationship through helping your client understand more clearly the dynamics of the relationship and identify more productive ways to manage it.

Case illustration

Sometimes this can be relatively straightforward as the following coaching scenario reveals. John, an executive client, has been in charge of a retail division for 12 months. David, his boss and a board director, has doubts about John's capability and is also frustrated that John rarely keeps him in the picture about his activities. This places David in awkward situations with the chief executive, Sally, because he often doesn't have sufficient accurate and detailed information at his fingertips about the performance of John's division. This reflects badly on him.

John, on the other hand, believes that he has been given a very senior job with a large salary and therefore should just get on with it. He thinks he will be bothering David if he burdens him with detailed information. He also fears that David would misinterpret information-giving as seeking to talk up his division and ingratiate himself. It doesn't cross his mind that David needs regular updating in order to feel adequately prepared for his performance review meetings with Sally.

During the coaching dialogue these thought patterns and relationship dynamics become evident to John and he quickly changes his communication pattern with David, offering far more information. David's perception also changes as he becomes more aware of what John and his division are actually achieving.

This scenario ends with a positive result but inevitably this will not always be the case. Some clients decide that they are not prepared to make the necessary adjustments or simply can't change themselves enough to conform to expectations. They then conclude that the only way is out and take preemptive action to find another job. They may, of course, not get that choice if the company arrives at that view more quickly than they do and instigates the exit process first.

Failure to build and lead a team

Effective team leadership is seen today as a core management competency. There is an expectation that senior managers and executives provide clear direction, communicate the vision, mission and values of the organisation and lead their teams towards achieving the organisation's agenda. This means selecting excellent people in the first instance, coaching them and developing a high-performance team ethos.

Sometimes, in order to create the strongest possible team it may be necessary to make changes in its membership. In this scenario there will be an expectation that the team leader takes the necessary action in a timely and effective manner. If the executive delays too long, then this can develop into a performance issue. Making sound appointments, removing underperformers and proactively building teams are key performance themes for executives and as a coach you need to be aware of them.

Emotional intelligence issues

Emotional intelligence is often cited as a key positive difference between good and great leaders. It is portrayed as an excellence factor – a set of qualities that helps people shine and stand out from their colleagues. The opposite side of this is that poor levels of emotional intelligence can now be a career-threatening factor. Historically, people with low self- and social awareness were often tolerated and colleagues found their ways of working around them. Nowadays that tolerance runs out more quickly in many organisations.

Managers whose moods, behaviours and outbursts negatively affect the morale of their teams are under increasing scrutiny. Insensitivity, manipulation, bullying, aloofness are just some of the behaviours that have become increasingly unacceptable in many companies. Team leaders are expected to inspire, motivate and set a positive emotional climate where people can perform at their best.

Emotional competence matters in other contexts too. Team leaders themselves are members of more senior teams and are regularly exposed to visitations from the highest management in the company. Individuals who lack relationship management skills stand out and if they embarrass, irritate or anger their seniors then trouble may not be far away.

Failure to meet business objectives

Failing to meet business objectives will inevitably be the most critical career-threatening performance issue. Sometimes as the coach you will be briefed about performance concerns of this kind but this is not always the case. It is common to be coaching individuals where serious questions exist about their capacity to meet key business objectives and for you not to know. Instead the first you realise it is when your client announces that she is in negotiations with the company about an exit package or when the telephone rings and it is the HR director explaining what has just happened.

This can leave you wondering how you didn't pick it up and perhaps angry that the company didn't choose to tell you about the seriousness of the situation. It may also raise the question in your mind like 'how come my client didn't realise it?'

There will rarely be a simple answer to this but there are some common scenarios. The first is that the organisation may not wish to share such sensitive information with someone outside of their boundaries and control. However trustworthy you believe you are, the company's top management may choose to keep their deliberations on a strictly need-to-know basis. Secondly, the company may not realise that there is a coach involved or may hold coaches in poor esteem. Thirdly, clients may have been deluding themselves and being deluded by their own senior management – they just didn't see it coming because their view was that they were performing well and delivering on their key business objectives.

There are ways that the coach can try to stay in the picture. Where you have close contact with the senior players in the company or have good access to the HR director there is more likelihood that key information will be shared. This is a further reason why the triangular contracting relationship can be so important in executive coaching. However, there is an inescapable truth in the life of the executive coach – the system will not always see you as a neutral ally to be consulted on matters to do with your work. Sometimes doors will be open to you and sometimes they will be kept firmly closed.

Leaving well

Executives inevitably react differently to the shock of being made redundant. For most it will be their first experience on the receiving end but there are some for whom it has happened before. Disbelief, sadness, anger and confusion are just a few of the feelings expressed at this time. Helping clients come through these episodes is an increasingly familiar aspect of the executive coaching role. This usually starts with encouraging clients to tell the story in detail, express their feelings as they need to, and begin to make more sense of what has happened and why.

In executive circles there is a view about how people are best advised to respond to this situation. Colleagues recognise that the news will be devastating in the first instance but also have an expectation that the manager recovers sufficient composure to deal with the exit process in a civilised manner. They are not comfortable with intense expressions of emotion and want to get the whole thing done as speedily as possible without a fight.

Most executives decide that it is in their own best interests to play it this way despite how they are feeling. They realise that they will probably need a good reference from the company to show to prospective employers and are careful not to sour relationships, which could affect future employment. They often want their coach to support them in this strategy and help them keep up an external appearance until negotiations are completed. It is common for these clients to report that their partners are angrier than they are with the company. Nevertheless they have decided that they want to 'leave well', and not under a cloud.

This is not always the case and some clients are just so furious with the organisation for turning their world upside down without warning that they make a fight over their dismissal. Their energies become fixed on legal action to address what they perceive to be a grave injustice. The client's focus changes and they perceive their solicitor as their main professional support. Situations of this kind can signal the end of the coaching relationship.

5　Personal development coaching

Getting closure around unfinished business

Unfinished business is one of the most common themes brought to coaching. This is a performance issue *par excellence* because it can be responsible for such a massive drain on an individual's energy, focus, commitment and motivation. One could only hazard a guess as to how many people are currently thinking of leaving their jobs due to unresolved issues with colleagues, or bosses or who have already left because they couldn't find a resolution to a key working relationship.

To complicate matters further, unfinished business may not even emanate from individuals' current employment. It may date back to negative experiences in a previous job. Nevertheless, the unresolved feelings from that situation now leak out in the current context, restimulated by similarities perceived by the individual in the here-and-now.

Some might say that this kind of material is best left alone; that there is an inherent danger in opening up these issues. Instead it's better to live with it. There is a viewpoint that this is the realm of therapy and counselling, not coaching.

Both these positions are understandable reactions to what is usually a daunting prospect. Some unfinished business leaves such a scar that it is difficult to see how the individual can ever move forward without skilled psychotherapeutic help. In these cases colleagues may have tried everything they know to help but with little success and have now given up or simply work around the person.

The cost is likely to be high for teams containing this sort of individual. They often exert an undermining influence on team morale and take an inordinate amount of management time. Typically, senior managers are desperate to find a solution and will have considered firing them. They may be reluctant to do so because the individual is not necessarily under-performing in the technical aspect of the job. And then there is the risk of an industrial tribunal further down the line.

Every organisation contains a number of individuals with serious unfinished business and there are usually many more stewing away with unfinished issues about a whole range of things from feeling devalued to being falsely accused of something. Executives and managers, often with the help of HR staff, are working through unfinished issues on a daily basis through private conversations, mediated processes, team away-days and residential retreats.

The prospect of taking on such issues, though daunting to people, is nevertheless something that managers and staff recognise must be done. The cost of not doing so is too high. Performance suffers and individuals either withdraw their full commitment or, in time, withdraw altogether to another company.

So what can coaching do in these circumstances – can it be an intervention that moves things on? Experience demonstrates that in many cases it can. The coach might be the first person to fully listen, without judgement or interruption, to the aggrieved person. Everyone else may be too involved in the issue to allow such individuals to tell their story in detail. And typically, telling it in detail is an absolutely essential first step. Surprising though this may seem, it sometimes takes little more than this. The experience of being really heard can be enough for some people to let go of their emotional investment and begin to see things differently.

Inevitably, it won't always be so. There is often a need for the individual to go around the issues on more than one occasion and where the problems lie in a present relationship, go back and speak to the main protagonist. It is common to find that clients have never really spoken directly to the person central to their issues. When the coach asks the obvious question – 'have you told him this?' – the answer is often no. Or, 'I've said some of it but not in this way.' Addressing unfinished business issues can sometimes be more productive when the coach uses relatively simple techniques that are aimed at discharge of emotion and rehearsal of what the client wants to say to the other person. Doing this in a safe space can often be the precursor for working through the issue later with the real person.

Developing emotional intelligence

There are some organisations where the concept of emotional intelligence (EI) is relatively unknown or little understood. However, for the most part, EI or EQ, as it is often known, is now firmly on the management and organisational map. Goleman (1996) and others who put it there are much appreciated by their HR, training, consultancy and coaching colleagues because its theory has provided a stronger justification for people-development interventions. For years trainers, facilitators and consultants have felt vulnerable to the hard-nosed manager who takes delight in challenging the reasons for giving up hard-pressed management time for 'touchy feeling' training or team development activities.

In coaching terms it would be somewhat unusual for clients to sit down at their first session and say 'I'm here because I want to improve my emotional intelligence'. However, if you coach for long enough, you will soon be confronted by EI issues in your work. They surface most often under the umbrellas of both leadership coaching and behavioural change.

Goleman's classic EI model contains the basic elements found in most offerings on the subject:

1   Self-awareness
 • Understanding your own thoughts and feelings and their effects on others
 • Accurate assessment of own strengths and limitations
 • A strong sense of self-worth

2   Social awareness
 • Capacity to empathise
 • Organisational awareness
 • Recognising and striving to meet the needs of both internal and external customers

3   Self-management
 • Ability to control potentially disruptive emotions and impulses
 • Adaptability
 • Achievement orientation
 • Self-motivation
 • Effective stress management

4   Relationship management
 • Ability to foster deep, lasting and meaningful relationships
 • Capacity to align others
 • Clear communication
 • Ability to inspire others
 • Capacity to influence change
 • Resolves conflict
 • Builds collaborative teams
 • Develops people

Some executive coaches view emotional intelligence as so central to their work that they have sought out additional training and accreditation in the use of EI assessment processes. The popularity of the subject has given rise to a plethora of self-rating and 360-degree tools that provide managers with a measurement of their emotional intelligence. As with any assessment instruments these have a place in coaching as they can provide rich, interesting and thought-provoking data. They can act as awareness raisers and may also have an immediate change impact.

One of the most positive messages from EI theory is that EI can be developed, a finding supported by many thousands of practitioners over recent decades who have worked with individuals and teams to promote awareness building and to improve interpersonal skills.

Those who specialise in the areas of leadership development and behavioural work will recognise the importance of emotional competence as an important vehicle for learning and change. As Wasylyshyn (2003) rightly notes: executives' abilities to change behaviour, increase self-understanding, and become more effective leaders to a large degree hinges on their making progress in one or more of the dimensions of emotional competence (self-awareness, self-management, social awareness and relationship management).

Coaching as a tool for EI development

Just as coaching is about change, whether that be in perspective, attitude or behaviour, it is also about helping people develop their EI. Often it's one and the same thing. Arguably, coaching for behavioural change is synonymous with coaching for EI development. Many behavioural change issues are to do with self- and social awareness, self-management and relationship skills.

The starting place for the development of emotional intelligence is awareness raising – clients becoming more aware of themselves and others. Undoubtedly one-one coaching can be an excellent process for facilitating this development and, on its own, can produce outstanding results. It also contains an inbuilt limitation. The very fact that there are only two people sitting in a room together means that external feedback for the client can only be derived from the coach. Of course this can be supplemented back in the workplace and wider life, but in the here and now of the coaching session, the range of opportunities for varied feedback is already defined.

For this reason, the group situation has much to commend it as a supplement to one-one coaching. My view is that the most productive approach to EI development involves a parallel process of individual coaching alongside experientially focused workshops or, better still, ongoing groups. This creates opportunities for clients to gain feedback from a number of people on their impact on others. This is also a context where people can practise tuning in to others as well as becoming more conscious of their own inner worlds.

For some clients the most challenging areas of EI development are in the self management and social awareness domains. It is not uncommon for clients to be acutely, and sometimes embarrassingly, aware of their shortcomings in these areas. They know that they soon run out of patience and can be prone to highly damaging angry scenes with colleagues and wish that they could develop better self-control. 'If only I could recognise the signs earlier and not get into the vicious spiral' is a sentiment shared by many with these particular issues.

The capacity to empathise with others can also present as a development issue to some. They find it difficult to connect emotionally with what is going on in others and fail to understand the intensity of feeling experienced by others. Coaching to develop empathy in the one-one context is a far from easy task and, again, the group situation may be more fruitful and productive. Clients can grapple and experiment with tuning in and can get feedback from others as to whether their connectedness is experienced as authentic.

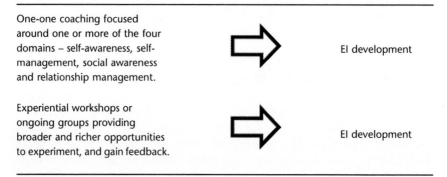

One-one coaching focused around one or more of the four domains – self-awareness, self-management, social awareness and relationship management.   ⇨   EI development

Experiential workshops or ongoing groups providing broader and richer opportunities to experiment, and gain feedback.   ⇨   EI development

Figure 5.1   Coaching for EI development.

In stressing the value of the group context we should not lose sight of the importance for many clients of the one-one situation. The safety, trust and confidentiality of the one-one are prized aspects of the coaching process and, in contrast, the group can appear intimidating and anxiety provoking. The joint approach will not suit everyone.

The EI of the coach

Up to now the focus has been confined to the development of EI in the client. Your emotional intelligence as the coach has been invisible, but not taken for granted. Many consultants, coaches, trainers and HR specialists are drawn to this topic but it doesn't follow that they possess high levels of emotional competence themselves. Indeed it can be quite the opposite. Practitioners may be attracted to the subject because they need to develop that competence themselves. The critical question is whether they are aware of this. If they aren't then there can be a gap between what they are espousing and how they are acting and this will inevitably diminish their presence. Those who do recognise their own developmental issues may be able to share their experience in ways that make them more accessible to their clients and thus easier to learn from.

The point is not that coaches require an exemplary level of EI, although this may be a worthwhile goal. Instead coaches need to work on themselves as well as working with other people.

Develop deeper self-belief and confidence

One of the most common insights shared by new coaches is how often the issues of self-belief and confidence feature in coaching. Perhaps the more interesting question is: 'why should we be so surprised?' After all, most of us are acutely aware of our own fears, anxieties and self-doubts. Why should we not expect to find those very same things in others? Yet often we fail to see it and instead make the assumption that others, particularly highly successful people, don't experience self-doubt to the same degree we do.

It may, of course, be well disguised. Senior people generally feel a pressure to perform, to look as if they know what they're doing and in control. Behind the public façade they may be struggling far more than they choose to show. The benefit of this performance can be that it shields them from questions and attention they don't wish to attract. The downside is that it gets in the way of support being offered.

There is also the issue of projection to take into account. If you unconsciously view people in leadership positions as special, different, and without the same needs you have, then you will treat them this way. You will miss their vulnerability, imagining that they are above these things. You may also be a little scared of them and back off even if you sense they may need something in that moment.

As coaches it's extremely important not to equate seniority and success with lack of need and invincible confidence. Some of the most outwardly successful people in all walks of life are beset by confidence issues. As a coach you can offer such clients an immensely valuable gift just by enabling them to share this with you without feeling judged.

6   Leadership coaching

Prepare for a future leadership role

Many organisations now take a proactive stance towards developing their future leaders and coaching is increasingly seen as a central part of that strategy. It is now commonplace for leadership development programmes to include individual coaching for all participants.

It is also typical for companies to use executive coaching as part of their succession planning and fast-tracking processes. Even those organisations who have traditionally given less priority to management development will often select a few up-and-coming individuals and provide them with an external coach to reinforce the learning from their executive development programmes.

More developmentally focused organisations have gone further still and some use coaching as the primary tool for leadership development. These companies sometimes offer coaching to all their senior management team and then cascade it down to other levels.

Coaching managers for future leadership roles can encompass any or all of the coaching themes outlined in this section but there are a small number that feature most often and in my experience they are: influencing skills, the capacity for strategic thinking and leadership presence.

Becoming a more effective leader

> Show me a leader who doesn't think they're a good judge of character or a good manager of people. But there are many who work day to day unaware of the feelings of their people or of the impact on their people of the decisions they make. I always thought I was a good manager. I involved people in the decision-making process and encouraged them to learn and take initiative. But I lacked feedback. I didn't really know how I was doing, particularly in the eyes of those who worked for me. That's why I looked for an executive coach. (Jim)

It is still the case that some organisations promote managers to senior leadership roles on the back of their technical abilities. This hardly guarantees that they will become great leaders and many never achieve this. They fail to understand and grasp the leadership role and stay within the comfort zone of operational tasks.

Those companies who have recognised this problem now go to great lengths to recruit people with leadership capability to their senior executive roles. They are looking for people who have vision, can communicate it and who possess the capacity to motivate people. They understand the critical role that leaders play in creating high performance organisational cultures.

Some of these leaders become the clients of executive coaches and typically look to coaching to provide that 'little extra something' that will move them forward. They often present as eager to learn and relish the opportunity to unpack issues and gain new insights. The agendas they bring encompass personal, team and strategic organisational issues. Their common coaching topics include business performance, change management, organisational politics, managing upwards and conflict resolution. The coach acts as a strategic partner and sounding board as the leader works on their own agenda.

As a coach you need to remember that coaching may be the only place in your clients' working life where they can reveal what is really happening for them. Role relationships can prevent executives sharing their difficult issues and the coaching dialogue may be their one and only safe, confidential space.

> I had known for some time that I needed support and that I was feeling isolated, but I had been too busy to do anything about it. I needed to talk to someone I could trust, someone I could share ideas with and someone outside of my immediate family. I realised that at certain times my confidence levels dropped as I had doubts about the way I was doing things. Coaching enabled me to explore and reframe, which led to me feeling differently as a result of just talking about it. I wouldn't have gone there on my own. (Janet)

In the early stages of the coaching relationship there will often be questions of trust and capability in the leader's mind about their coach. Will the coach understand me and my world? Can the coach handle me? Can she provide what I need? Do I really even know what I'm looking for?

Different issues are brought by clients at different stages of their leadership careers. New leaders often grapple with the whole question of what leadership is about and what kind of leaders they want to be. It can be useful for you to explore this with your clients as they may have never before considered these questions in any real depth. Identifying role models from both the public domain and those within your client's organisation can help this process. The client may also find it helpful to be pointed in the direction of some leadership literature. Some coaches keep stocks of management and leadership books around so that they can offer specific texts to meet the different needs of their clients.

The issues involved in coaching well-established leaders can be different. Whereas the new leader may still be in the self-conscious stage wondering whether they are really up to it and concerned about making the right impression, the seasoned leader may have different questions on his mind. Working with the new leader may be about confidence-building; the experienced leader may be getting bored or wondering if he has really made a difference to his organisation.

People who operate at executive level generally have to cope with volume, speed and complexity. They learn to manage a schedule that many would find daunting. They start early, finish late and in between are bombarded with stimuli from all directions. This has a stressful dimension to it, but it also provides excitement and interest value. Operating in this executive fast lane can result in a need for regular fixes of something new and if these don't come along fast enough then they can get bored and restless. This scenario sends alarm bells around senior colleagues who often spot the signs and get anxious at the prospect of either interference in their patch or the boss setting up new ventures to satisfy his need for action.

Keeping fresh and stimulated is certainly an important issue for experienced leaders and is a recurrent theme in coaching. Some executives replenish themselves by seeking out new learning experiences such as executive development programmes. Others find a platform for themselves and set up speaking engagements at national or international conferences. Networking with colleagues from other organisations and sitting on strategic partnership forums are also favoured activities.

Leader as coach

Increasingly, modern leaders recognise their role as coaches to their own senior teams. Some go further and act as sponsors for coaching within their organisations. When leaders take on a more coaching style of leadership it can give them a new lease of life. They enjoy the opportunity to connect more meaningfully with their colleagues and take pleasure in playing a significant role in the personal growth and development of their people.

In the early stages, leaders are not always confident about taking on a coaching style and question whether they have the skill sets to do a good job. They may therefore welcome the opportunity to undertake some training. This in turn can result in a growing consciousness that the people development aspect of leadership is what they enjoy most and some become so enthusiastic that they progress to advanced level coaching development. They then use this learning back in their companies and some go on to become executive coaches themselves following retirement.

Develop influencing skills

> I'm confident in my own technical knowledge and when I have to represent my own department. But I don't tend to contribute much to corporate debates or when one of the other directors is speaking about their area. I'm actually rather a shy person and I don't like talking just for the sake of it. I probably underestimate what I could contribute. I'm also not very confident about challenge so I hold back. The fact is I don't really have a lot of impact in senior management meetings and I keep getting that feedback from the Chief Executive who wants me to get more involved. (Paul)

One of the most common developmental needs emerging for new leaders and those aspiring to leadership positions is the capacity to influence and have impact. From a coaching perspective it is one of the most interesting and yet challenging issues to coach on. Take a moment and ask yourself how you might work with someone to develop that person's influencing skills and improve their leadership impact. You may have begun to think about what gives people a higher or lower level of personal influence. Who do you know who has it? How did they acquire it? Is it about personality, style and presence? What influences you? How do you influence?

For the coach there are several ways to explore influence and impact with a client. The first is to ask some of the above questions. It will probably be helpful for clients to clarify what is meant by influence and impact. They may have received some feedback about how people perceive them and this will be worth exploring for common themes and messages. Are they too quiet or self-demeaning? Are they seen as belligerent or self-opinionated? What do they know about their presence and what, if anything, do they want to change or develop?

Role models provide a rich source of learning. It can be helpful for clients to identify people in their organisations who exhibit the desired characteristics. Simply identifying those traits can be a valuable awareness-raising exercise in itself. From here it can be productive for clients to spend some time with their role models and try to get behind how they think and behave.

There is another method open to the coach and that is the use of the here and now relationship between the coach and client. In other words as the coach you invite your clients to receive feedback on the impact they are having on you during the ongoing process of the coaching relationship. This is a very direct and powerful method as the clients gain immediate feedback on their characteristic styles of relating and behaviours.

The final method is shadowing, another direct and very potent way of providing feedback on influence and impact. On a number of occasions I coached executives at my coaching premises and formed a particular impression only to find later, when I observed them in their work settings, that I had completely missed some key information. I may have initially thought they communicated well, were relatively comfortable with themselves and would have no trouble holding their own in executive circles. To my surprise I later found that they were noticeably different around their bosses and peers. Shadowing provides an excellent opportunity to notice influencing in practice. It throws up a wealth of rich data from which to provide feedback and to frame experimentation with new behaviours.

Becoming more strategic

> I have always known that I was good at my job from an operational perspective, but deep down I knew I'd always had difficulty with the strategic aspect – basically because I could not let go. I did not feel able to trust my team to deliver and consequently tried to do everything myself. This wasted time and resources and effectively I took my eye off the ball by having too much focus on the wrong issues. (Jennifer)

The capacity to think strategically has been seen as a high-value competency for some time. Many senior managers still feel more comfortable at the operational level and have a tendency to get overinvolved with the detail. This typically frustrates both their bosses and subordinates.

The word 'strategy' scares some of these managers. They privately worry that they will one day be exposed as not knowing what it really means or how to do it. Helping a client learn how to be strategic can therefore be a valuable coaching contribution. This implies, of course, that the coach has a good appreciation of strategy, which may not always be the case. It can be an important development area for some executive coaches too. With this in mind the following thoughts may be equally valuable to the coach for your own learning as they are when you are coaching an executive who wants to become more strategic.

The expression *bigger picture* is often used when describing strategic thinking but what does this mean? In essence it refers to getting out of the detail, rising above it and analysing issues from a broader perspective. A key aspect of this perspective is to see patterns in events. Strategically focused executives scan their business environment to identify emerging patterns both within her own industry or field and across related ones that might have an impact on them. The well-known SWOT analysis is often used as a structured method for doing this. This process focuses attention on Strengths, Weaknesses, Opportunities and Threats.

Companies and executives who read the signals quickly and make effective decisions based on early identification often get in front of the game – those who don't run the risk of falling behind. So how do people develop this ability to spot important trends and then formulate successful responses to them?

Put simply it is about looking up and looking out and doesn't happen when our heads are down. Looking out can be achieved through networking: an activity much encouraged in executive life. Some managers seem to be naturals at it; others hate it. It requires pushing past inhibitions and shyness – something that managers with a more introverted personality often struggle with. Difficult though it may be for some, it is obvious that an executive with a wide-ranging network of strong interpersonal relationships will pick up a great deal more environmental information than the one who doesn't have this.

How, then, can executive clients develop their capacity to think strategically? As a coach this is something you need to consider as you will be regularly confronted by the question. A good place to start is to ask your clients who strikes them as bigger-picture thinkers in their own company. Usually they will immediately come up with one or two names. Further probing will reveal what it is about these people that put them into this category. The clients may then seek these people out and spend some time with them to get behind how they think and see the world.

Another powerful learning environment for strategic thinking is participation in higher level meetings and strategic projects. Clients may need to volunteer more often when these kinds of opportunities come around. Back in their own operational teams they might also learn much of value from involving staff in brainstorms or more informal discussions about trends and patterns.

Learning the art of asking good questions, one of coaching's main tools, can also be invaluable to those learning what it means to think more strategically. Executives might practise with their own teams by asking such questions as:

- What do we already know that we will finally act on in a year's time?
- How is our business environment changing?
- What are our main competitors doing that we might do too?
- What are the essential ingredients of our success?
- What single thing would most move us forward as a company?
- What should we be doing now to stay ahead of the game in the future?

These are just a few ways to improve strategic capacity and this is an area where executive clients will perceive high added value if you can help them make significant strides.

Create a high-performance team and organisation

Many CEOs and managing directors share a similar desire – to lead a high-performance senior team and organisation. They often use their coaching to explore how this can be achieved. This can be a fascinating yet at the same time seductive coaching agenda for many coaches. If you have been a senior executive yourself you will have probably shared the same aspiration and may be tempted to use your clients as proxies for your own unrequited ambitions. Similarly, former HR directors, management trainers and OD consultants may find themselves strongly invested in the outcomes of their client's endeavours. All of this has its positive side. You are likely to be highly engaged and motivated. The danger is that there can be a temptation to slip into the role of expert and begin to dispense your views on how you would go about developing the team or changing the organisation.

Some clients may be keen to hear the coach's suggestions and may be content to change the focus to a consultancy session. Executives tend to be pragmatists and if they can get some useful thinking from the coach most will want to take it. Just as there will be times when a coaching session veers towards counselling, such as when personal issues are predominant, so there will be other occasions when a liberal dispensation of consultancy advice is in order. The issue, as ever, is to be vigilant about how much, how often, and what effect it's having on the coaching process.

Most senior executives yearn for a high-performance team but few ever have the privilege of leading one. This is not necessarily a reflection on their own team leadership, although this will always be a factor; rather, such teams are a genuine rarity at the top of organisations. Individual accountability tends to take precedence over collective accountability and team members are not always persuaded that taking the risks to trust and be open is worth the gamble.

One of the stronger reasons why you will feel very engaged in the high-performance agenda is that you may believe that coaching itself offers such a powerful and effective route to achieve the goal. Many companies now share this view and have embarked on coaching culture initiatives. We have yet to see whether research vindicates the high expectations placed on this form of organisational intervention.

Staying relatively neutral, then, and not entering the arena as a player, can be an issue when it comes to this theme. The coach with a strong organisational change and development background may have much to offer and the client may be eager to receive it.

7 Meaning-making

Coaching themes are inextricably linked to stages of life. The emotional as well as life tasks and challenges facing us at 20, 40 and 60 years old can be significantly different. In the early stage of our careers most of us are concerned with getting a foot on the ladder and then making progress. We are eager to learn our craft and perform sufficiently well in our work to make a good impression. There are many other important things going on outside of work especially in our relationship world. As our careers progress and we grow older, new career goals often replace those initial ones. We start to ask questions about how far we can go and where we want to go. In the third stage those questions tend to change and focus more around whether we have derived satisfaction and fulfilment from our work.

Executive coaches tend to work with people in the second and third stages of their careers. Clients are usually in their mid-30s through to late 50s. Some will therefore be more concerned with building their careers and others may be looking back, reevaluating and considering retirement or a consultancy career. Coaching issues, then, are often stage specific.

This is not to say that questions relating to satisfaction and contribution only arise when the hair begins to recede or grey. Many younger executives in their late 30s and 40s have well worked-out plans to leave corporate life by the time they reach 50 or even earlier. Some of these people earn substantial salaries and bonuses, which make a retirement age of 45 perfectly feasible.

Meaning-making issues

A range of issues can bring on the need to make greater sense and meaning of our work and wider lives. Those that belong to our personal lives are outside the scope of this book although it is important to note that clients will refer to these. Those that more directly relate to the work context tend to be about contribution, values, wholeness, work/life balance, health, satisfaction or a desire to try something completely different.

When executives raise these sorts of issues it can be from a life position of mild curiosity to one of serious crisis. Clients may recognise that they are noticing the toll executive life is taking on them. They comment on how little time they have for themselves and their families. They are often acutely aware of the cost on their primary relationships and the long-term danger to their health. But, in their minds, it is still an issue for the future. They are feeling the heat but it's bearable. They also acknowledge that this is the price to be paid for financial security later in life as well as school fees now.

In contrast there are some executives who have gone well past this mark. They are now experiencing a major crisis of meaning in relation to their work. This can be precipitated by career derailment in terms of losing their job or being passed over for promotion several times. Inevitably these scenarios throw up massive questions for executives who begin to question their previous colleague relationships, whether they were really valued, and whether they were told the truth.

One of the most profound and potentially disturbing scenarios that can contribute to a crisis of meaning is when a long-established boss relationship turns sour. Very rarely does the full story ever come out, which leaves the individual feeling hurt, distress and confusion. They simply can't get to the bottom of what went wrong.

Work/life balance

For most people the issue of work/life balance is an inescapable truth of their lives. Executives typically see it as part of the deal. They are highly aware that they are over-extended but accept the trade-off. Some make valiant attempts to get home at a sensible hour and attempt to role model this with colleagues; many more live with excessively long hours and staggeringly large workloads.

A senior executive client who recently parted company with his organisation wryly commented to me: 'Well the good news is that I'll finally be able to spend some time with my family. That side of my life has suffered in recent years. I wonder whether they'll recognise me.' Another client, a managing director with strong career ambitions, remarked at the outset of the coaching: 'There are three priorities in my life – work, golf and my family. And they're in that order.' You may be interested to know that the rank order had changed by the end of the coaching. At a senior team-development workshop he reflected to his colleagues on what he had told me earlier. 'Now it's family, work and then golf.' They were pleased to hear it but remained a little sceptical.

Coaching sessions very often focus on this whole question of how to create a better balance between work and wider life. From a change perspective clients are often still in the contemplation stage of the change process as defined by Prochaska (1994). It's nagging at them but they may not be ready to make the changes required to make a difference. You will usually be able to empathise from your own version of this issue.

Contribution

At some point in most people's lives the issue of making a contribution rises to the surface. We may have been busy building our careers, families, and financial security for later in life now to find that a different question dominates our thinking. There can be a number of variations of it such as the following:

- What am I giving back?
- What contribution am I making to the world?
- How can I put something back in?
- How can I give my time and experience to others to help them?

These are some of the existential issues facing many of us. They often revolve around our purpose and the legacy we wish to leave. Theses themes and questions are common when coaching people who are just reaching or who have now entered the second half of their lives. They are about finding meaning.

Integration

In order to succeed in our careers we can think that certain aspects of ourselves may need to take a back-seat or even be hidden altogether. When we are younger we do not have the life experience to know what will be and won't be acceptable in the work environment. For example, we may surmise that to be seen as professional we need to curtail some of our creative, wilder side. We may consciously project certain aspects of our personalities whilst simultaneously rejecting or disowning other parts.

This is perfectly understandable as nobody is given a rule book that includes a chapter on 'How you can be at work'. Everyone has to find their own way on it. Some people get lucky and are encouraged by their manager and fellow team members to be themselves. Mostly people study what seems to be acceptable and adapt accordingly. These adaptations may prove to be functional in helping learn how to negotiate corporate life but can, in time, bend people out of shape.

The heftiest and most challenging existential questions can then lay in waiting. Who am I? Am I my corporate identity? Am I more than that?

Some, though not all, clients bring these questions to their sessions. They are seeking to understand the impact on them of their leadership roles and to rediscover who they are and what they want from their life. This process invariably involves reclaiming aspects of self that have been put aside.

One of the great influencers of psychological thought, Erikson (1959), referred to the eight stages of life as containing particular psychosocial and developmental challenges. The latter stage, when people are moving towards retirement and beyond, is a stage characterised by the issue of integrity versus despair. If we are able to find personal meaning and satisfaction from our life and work then a sense of integrity will prevail. If we cannot, and instead see our work and life as unfulfilled, then we may experience a feeling of despair.

This may look as if we have crossed the border into therapy. However these are common issues for people in the second half of their lives and coaches need to be conscious that there will be occasions when their clients will want to discuss them. You do not need to feel that you have to fix anything. How can you anyway? What you can do is to remind your clients of what they have achieved and the innate goodness they possess. Coaches can also help their clients find those disowned parts of themselves and become more whole in themselves. If coaching is not producing that deeper process of integration then this may signal a need to refer on to a counsellor. This may happen from time to time, but most clients will simply value the opportunity to voice their issues about the meaning of their working lives.

Concluding thoughts

Experienced executive coaches know full well that coaching conversations around meaning-making issues such as those described above can lead to a range of outcomes. Very often they enable clients to achieve a sense of purpose, clarity and positive recognition of achievement and worth. On a few occasions that clarity will be more to do with deciding that the current work situation is wrong for them. The coaching process gives them a place to reflect and the outcome is a decision to leave.

When the coaching is being sponsored by the organisation, and in the case of executive coaching it normally will be, this can raise a difficult issue. However most organisational sponsors of coaching understand this risk and many coaches ensure that the subject is raised at the contracting stage. Usually, if the client is so unaligned to the values of the organisation or the way it is heading then it is in the best interests of both sides if an amicable departure is the final outcome.

PART 3
The foundations of a psychological approach to coaching

8 The key dimensions of a coaching session

The key dimensions of a coaching session are:

1 The client's story.
2 The emotional level – the client's feeling.
3 The cognitive level – the client's thinking.
4 The coach's use of self.

1 The client's story

In reviewing my own coaching experience over the years, and having witnessed many hundreds of hours of practice sessions conducted by coaches in training, I find that there is invariably a story the client wishes to tell. It may simply be background for a performance issue or a complex and intricate tale that the client thinks you must understand in order to be helpful. Experienced coaches tend to manage the storytelling as they know that they need fewer facts than the client tends to believe. Less experienced coaches can fall into the trap of believing they must understand all aspects of the story and sometimes become worried about losing elements of it. It is important that aspiring coaches learn the skill of tracking issues, but getting hooked and hypnotised by the story is something to avoid. The coach can also be prone to other self-interference such as being anxious to ask good questions and keep the session moving at a good pace. This can lead to the danger of rehearsing the next question instead of really listening to what is being said now.

Good coaching is a dialogue rather than an interview, with a looser and more flexible rhythm. This requires the coach to relax, let go of fixed ideas of where the session should go and work more with emerging needs and process. Part of the emerging process is the impact that clients and indeed the session are having on the coaches, and this is what is known as using the self as instrument of change.

The importance of the client's story

Although you should be careful not to get lost in the story it is nevertheless important to remember how significant it is to the client. This may be especially true where clients are unable to share difficult issues with anyone else in the workplace due to their leadership role. Other clients may have an intolerable situation at home or problems at work that cannot be addressed elsewhere. These issues may have been split off, unable to be addressed and sapping energy, yet with no outlet.

Just having the opportunity to talk it out with good attention from the coach can be therapeutic in itself. It meets a deep psychological need to be heard. Listening to their own story as they tell it can also enable clients to see their issues in a different light.

Many people are starved of opportunities to get things off their chest with someone listening well to them. As a coach you should never underestimate the value of simply hearing someone out. If you can do that without judgement, better still. Clients may only recognise the burden they have been carrying once they have shared their story with an accepting listener.

Coaching and counselling experience over the years has shown that there is not just a therapeutic value from being deeply listened to. Very often people resolve their problems, issues and conflicts through this process without significant intervention. This is the basis of the client-centred philosophy.

> A large part of the role that a coach undertakes is to listen and reflect, not to attempt to answer questions that they are not qualified to answer. My coach knew me very well from the work he had been involved with in the business. He also was well aware of the people and the issues. It must have been tempting for him to jump straight to what he perceived to be the core problem. But he knew, and I came to know, that what was important to me was to realise the core issue for myself and develop a solution to take matters forward. Mostly I was able to do this. (Jim)

The dangers of only working with the client's story

Working at the level of the client's story will often be enough. However, this won't always be the case. Clients may find themselves going round the same old thinking that they have already done inside their own heads or spoken about before and there may be a sense of stuckness or impasse. The clients may be bored hearing themselves say the same old things and may experience the listening and support of the coach as only mildly useful. In this situation there is a need for something else to happen. If it doesn't, then the clients can lose interest, energy and commitment to the process. They may say it was good to talk and that the coach was friendly, supportive and empathetic but the session didn't crack the important issues, or even identify them in the first place.

Another danger of being story-focused is that you can get sucked in and lose your own sense of perspective. Worse still, if the story is a negative one and clients have little optimism about being able to improve or change their situation, then you can get dragged down into a sense of hopelessness. This can then set off the following sorts of reaction in the coach: a desire to fix things, an urgency to get a result before it has really presented itself, or a feeling of helplessness and inadequacy.

When you feel these things you have probably lost your ground and may experience yourself as thrashing around for a while. Interestingly, this can be a highly productive place to be, although it rarely feels that way. Sometimes the answer is to use these experiences, your inner process, as a source of data and intervention – the use of self.

But before exploring that, there are two further levels to the coaching process that enable the coach to get beyond the client's story. These are clients' cognitive and emotional processes – how they are constructing their view of the world and how they are feeling about it.

Going beyond the story

Working with clients' thinking processes is about examining the way they think, especially when it might be limiting their wellbeing, fulfilment and success. Peltier (2001) makes the important point that a 'coach can (and should) tell you that you are thinking poorly, while few others can do this. Your spouse can't, your colleagues can't, and your boss can't either.'

However this raises some uncomfortable questions such as what faulty thinking is and who is to judge. Is this placing the coach in the role of arbiter of sound and unsound thinking?

Clearly it is not. Coaches always need to be aware of the danger of imposing their own world views, values and judgements on their clients. Their task is not to pass opinion on the rights and wrongs but to reflect back to the client how they are seeing and experiencing their situation. This creates the potentiality for clients to assess more clearly the quality of their own thinking. Ultimately the choice and decision-making, not only about action (or inaction) but also about what meaning to derive from the situation, must lie with the client. Very often clients know that their own thinking patterns can be the source of problems. A number of client perspectives may be helpful here to illustrate the point:

I get a lot of feedback about being too laid-back. I need to be more assertive and challenging as a manager because my performance is not what it should be but I really don't like conflict. I try to be Mr Nice all the time because I think being challenging will inevitably lead to conflict. I know, deep down, that I won't necessarily be seen as Mr Nasty if I challenge but that's my fear so I avoid it. (Danny)

When I see the world as threatening, which I often do, I get into 'battler' mode. Then I invariably get into a fight with someone, usually my boss. It often happens when I think something is unfair. Then I think to myself that someone has to stand up for what's right and it may as well be me. I believe that I'm not being authentic unless I take a stand. Later I usually find that I've built something up too much and it wasn't as serious as I'd first thought. But it's too late, the damage is done. I really have got to get my thinking straightened out earlier. It's all just too tiring. (Sarah)

I feel as if I must succeed all the time so I spend far more energy and time on things than they need or is good for me. I've realised that beneath all this I have a core belief which is that you're only as good as your last achievement. I'm always feeling insecure yet I know that actually people rate me very highly. They'd probably tell me to calm down and relax if they only knew. I would, if it was one of my staff. (Barry)

2 The cognitive level – the client's thinking processes

We all see the world in our own way. How often do we use the phrase 'the reality is' when we are really talking about our view of reality. We can then be shocked, dismayed, confused or angry when others don't act in accord with our expectations. Despite life experience demonstrating to us that our own thinking can be as faulty as the next person's we sometimes act as if our perspective is the only true one.

How to challenge thinking

Self-evidently, clients may experience a challenge to their thinking as criticism or an attack, particularly if it is delivered ineptly. Challenging someone on their thinking needs to be done thoughtfully and skilfully if it is to have the desired effect and not simply push that individual into defensiveness. This is where it is important to gauge your client's desire and tolerance for challenge. Some clients expect it, even demand it. Others may see it as impertinent, even outrageous.

A good starting point is to act from a stance of interested curiosity. In other words you adopt a slightly detached, non-judgemental position of wanting to understand more about how the client comes to see the world in their own unique way. This is not with the intent of trying to change the client, which will most certainly produce resistance or shallow compliance, but more from the spirit of genuine enquiry.

If, as a coach, you have too much investment in achieving a particular outcome or result then you may be in danger of leading too strongly and this will surely be picked up by your client. Your job is to get your clients more interested and curious about their own inner process through raising self-awareness. The objective is to encourage them to see and hear themselves better by acting as a sounding board for them.

Returning to the question of resistance, it will generally be more productive to acknowledge the positive as well as negative aspects of any so-called faulty thinking. Busy managers who soak up their staff's problems may feel overloaded but there will usually be a positive side. Their staff will probably feel well looked after, cared for and genuinely helped. This will probably result in the manager being seen very positively and in turn will have implications for attempts to change behaviour as there is a payoff from staying in the same pattern.

Building psychological muscle

One of the great contributions to working at the cognitive level has been made by Kegan (1994) in his book *In Over Our Heads – The Mental Demands of Modern Life*. The particular relevance of his theory for coaches is that transformation takes place when we develop the ability to step back and reflect on something that used to be taken for granted yet now enters our consciousness in a way that allows us to make new decisions about it. This requires in Kegan's view a movement from what he calls 'Subject' to 'Object'. 'Subject' is the state where things are experienced as unquestioned simply because they are the very lenses through which we see life. They are taken for granted as true – they are our reality.

'Object', on the other hand, refers to things that are now in fuller awareness and can be seen, thought about, questioned and acted upon in a new way. This enables individuals to appreciate their beliefs, assumptions, relationship issues, and aspects of their personality in a more objective light.

An example of the Subject/Object change would be Jane, a woman brought up in a family where her brother was expected and actively encouraged to go to university and follow a career path and she was constantly told 'just do your best – you can always get a job as a secretary.'

This message left a deep and lasting impact on Jane to the point where she simply didn't ever really consider herself as capable of achieving a management position. It just became her unquestioned reality. Later when she was given the opportunity to go on a personal development course she discovered that she had never even realised that she had been seeing her life in this way. She was shocked at how she had taken on a set of expectations and lived them out. She then had to decide whether to remain as a secretary or to go for promotion and start to build a long-term career. What mattered to her was that she finally felt that she was deciding the course of her life.

Personal growth and development is about moving more and more from 'Subject' to 'Object' and, as we increasingly do this, our capacity for dealing with complexity and change grows. We can see, reflect on, be responsible for, and act on more things. Kegan refers to this as building greater 'psychological muscle'. In a rapidly changing and ever more complex world this can be seen as a critical goal for executive coaching.

Relevance to the coach

It is common for executives and senior managers to assume unquestioningly that their worldview is accurate and largely shared by others. This is often revealed in failed change management initiatives, which fall on the rocks of resistance to change. From the so-called resistors' viewpoint they simply do not share the same view of reality.

At the individual level this can happen in developmental processes such as 360-degree feedback when managers' own views of themselves contrast sharply with those working around them. In this case, recipients of the feedback may be unprepared or unable to take on board the messages coming from colleagues as they do not conform to their own self-assessment.

Conversely, these sorts of processes can help someone to get a new perspective though it may not endure unless sufficient effective support and challenge continues into the future. Initially, individuals may open up to what is being said and grapple with a perspective which is not their own. Out of this they may gain new insights and make decisions and commitments to address developmental issues. However, if they don't build that 'psychological muscle' then there can be a tendency to stray back to previously held beliefs and assumptions and, in so doing, continue to evoke and elicit the same responses in others.

For the coach there are some clear messages here. Firstly, people do not change something until they first become aware of it – i.e. they move from being in it to being able to see and understand it. This is the movement from 'Subject' to 'Object'. So one of the key aspects of your role as coach is to facilitate heightened awareness in clients of the lenses through which they see the world and themselves.

Beyond this lies the somewhat daunting task of confronting those fixed views and assumptions to build greater flexibility and creativity into how the individual thinks. This requires courage as well as skill and understanding on your part and is something many executives want and expect from their coach. Taking the decision to grasp more strongly this aspect of the role can mean two things. Firstly, you may need to learn more about what is really involved in helping others to let go of assumptions and beliefs that may have contributed to why they have been successful.

Secondly, you may need to go back to yourself and ask some important questions about how comfortable you are with raising the level of challenge with your clients. Some coaches are wary of this, fearing their clients might reject their challenge and get defensive. They also worry that this may weaken trust and rapport. The danger is that if you stay too safe, adopt an overly supportive role and avoid taking risks then opportunities for new insight and growth may be lost.

Sometimes the most significant learning from the entire coaching process arises from that moment when you as the coach take the risk of really challenging your client on something that matters. When you reflect later, perhaps at the end of the process on your work together, it can be just these moments of truth that stand out as *the* transformative and pivotal experiences.

3 The emotional level – the client's feelings

When clients arrive at the key issues concerning them there will usually be an emotional dimension. Coaches can sometimes miss this or be unsure about whether to go there. One aspect of this confusion is that *feelings work* can seem like counselling or therapy and many coaches are not clear about where the boundary lies. For some coaches it is more personal than this. They are simply uncomfortable themselves with emotional expression and consciously try to shut it down.

Facilitating expression of emotion

It is entirely appropriate on occasions to facilitate emotional expression in the coaching context. Sometimes it is the very breakthrough that is urgently needed in order for the client to get unstuck and move on. Whatever you think and feel about this, it is inevitable that clients will bring their feelings into the room from time to time. This will certainly be the case when the client arrives at a session in a crisis situation such as career anxiety or derailment.

More common are those sessions that focus on confidence and

self-esteem issues, which can typically feature clients taking an overly self-critical view of themselves. Strong feelings of fear, anger, disappointment, hurt and frustration are commonplace in organisations and managers regularly bring these to their coaching. Recognising these feelings and having the opportunity to ventilate them can be enormously important for clients, particularly those who typically bottle things up or who have nowhere else safe enough to express them.

Nevertheless the message here is not to go 'hunting' emotions. Allowing and supporting the discharge of feelings when they naturally arise is all that may be necessary or appropriate.

It is worth noting that if every session is dominated by strong emotional discharge then that would be an indication that the client's needs are more suited to the counselling situation and it may be necessary to discuss the possibility of seeing a counsellor or therapist in the short term.

4 The coach's use of self

Though little discussed in the coaching literature to date I regard the use of self as *the* highest order coaching skill. It can be the key difference between good and great coaching. An elusive concept and very often difficult to communicate both to students and more experienced coaches, it is nonetheless a crucial aspect of any coaching professional's potency and wisdom. Why is it so elusive, so difficult to distil into a few easy phrases? Possibly because we are now in the territory of being able to say what it is you know and put words around those intuitive moments when you believe you know something but struggle to describe it. We all have these moments, although we may not always trust them enough to risk articulation. Later we might say to ourselves 'I knew there was something. I was picking it up . . . I wish I'd said something.' So you might simply feel at a loss to describe your inner experience and hold back. Other times you might put your thought into words but feel clumsy at descriptions that somehow still miss the mark and don't seem quite right. Finally, you may feel disempowered by your own reactions as demonstrated in the case notes of this trainee coach describing a practice session on her advanced coach training programme:

> When I found out that I would be coaching Dave, my heart sank! Having chatted to him socially and having observed him being coached in another session, I felt there was little or no chance of me being able to penetrate his defences. I knew I would have to work really hard to get anywhere and was apprehensive about how the session would go – not a good place to start from! My fears were realised. During the session, we 'danced' around each other – me

trying to get Dave to open up and him blocking my every move – the session finished with little prospect, I felt, of Dave making any changes to his work/life balance. I felt frustrated.

I realised afterwards, when I was receiving feedback, that when I had challenged Dave, it actually felt wrong to do so. I felt like I was back in school and I was telling my teacher that he was wrong – something you didn't do. And yet, here I was a mature, assertive, professional person who, in my everyday working life, would not have tolerated the lack of response to my direct questions. My realisation of the effect that Dave had had on me, made me understand, all too well, how valuable it would have been to tell him of the impact he was having on me and what a powerful tool the use of self would have been in that situation. My feeling about the whole session was if he was having that effect on me, what effect he has on people who are less mature, less assertive and so on. If I had offered how I was feeling at the time, perhaps Dave would have begun to 'see the light'! It was a session I shall not forget in a hurry and will be a valuable learning experience for future coaching sessions.

The learning here is that the very dynamics occurring in the coaching relationship may be a mirror image of clients' experiences in their workplace relationships – and they may be completely unaware of it.

The key questions for the coach are about how, if and when to use these internal data. Skilfully delivered, at the right time, these insights can be the most profound of all coaching interactions.

A source of your own self-interference as a coach can be your confusion over whether you are saying more about yourself than the client. Are you hijacking the client's agenda rather than offering something that may be helpful? For you to trust your internal radar you need to have a high degree of awareness of your own personal material, patterns and issues. This is the reason why self-development is such a crucial aspect of coaching development. Knowing, for example, whether your typical response to authority is challenge, compliance or avoidance of contact alerts you to whether your response in the here and now may be more to do with you than your client. The whole area of use of self as instrument is a complex yet fascinating one and is an ongoing theme of this book.

Summary

For the client, the coaching space is often a thinking space. It's a time to reflect, get clearer about issues and make decisions that feed into more effective action. It can be the time, perhaps the only time, when some clients feel able to tell their story and express their worries without fear of judgement and criticism. It can also be a time to celebrate successes and have someone recognise and validate hard-won achievements.

For the coach, the capacity to work at all four levels – the story, the client's thought processes and feelings, and the use of self – is undoubtedly a challenging proposition. If you are a newer coach then it may seem aspirational. Even experienced coaches often struggle to rise above the story and do what Gallwey (2000) refers to as 'eavesdropping' on someone's thinking and feeling processes. To do these and then add the fourth dimension of the skilful use of self requires a good deal of practice, personal examination and sense of timing.

If you are still practising the art of coaching the story and have yet to move to the other levels, take heart. The very fact that the client is heard and accepted is like being placed in sunlight. A crucial aspect of coaching from the client's perspective is to feel respected, understood and acknowledged.

9 Psychological mindedness – the foundation stone of psychological competence

Psychological mindedness

Whether executive coaching is defined as primarily about learning or change, and arguably they are one and the same thing, my contention is that coaches require a certain level of psychological skill and competence to operate effectively across the wide range of assignments likely to come their way. The foundation stone of this competence is psychological mindedness.

Psychological mindedness, as a term, was not invented in coaching. Like so many of coaching's concepts it has been borrowed from elsewhere – in this case psychotherapy. The term has found its way into coaching literature recently through Lee (2003) in his book on leadership coaching. There is also an increasing use of the concept when describing the higher level competency categories of executive coaching. Purchasers of coaching increasingly see psychological mindedness as the top-level competence they seek in executive coaches, along with business knowledge and coaching excellence. Its meaning is not technically exact and it is more usefully seen as an umbrella concept that refers to people's *capacity to reflect on themselves, others, and the relationship between*. It is rooted in a curiosity about how people tick and why we behave as we do. Furthermore it is about our ability to see the past in the present and make links between current issues and what has happened previously.

In essence it means to consider more deeply the causes and meanings of behaviour, thoughts and feelings. It is important to note, however, that there is a significant difference here between a lively curiosity about people and relationships and an obsessive reflection about oneself and one's psychological processes. The latter is not helpful in the coach and will almost definitely alienate many executive clients who may interpret it as excessive 'navel gazing'.

As a trainer of coaches and consultants I consider the first objective in the psychological competence journey is to help coaches develop their psychological mindedness. New coaches are often keen to acquire skills and techniques before building this essential platform. If you don't acquire this foundation then your work with clients may remain at the level of problem solving or, far more important, risk the opening up of deep-rooted issues through the unskilled application of potentially powerful developmental tools and techniques.

Some coaches-in-training can be impatient to get to the finishing line as quickly as possible and look for processes to use with their clients. They recognise that psychological mindedness implies a deeper reflection on self yet are reluctant to take on their own personal growth agendas out of a fear of what might be uncovered. This is perfectly understandable and not at all unusual. Many people coming into coaching have not undertaken in-depth personal development processes such as therapy and counselling. They imagine that if they take the lid off their own material they might be overwhelmed.

Lee (2003) is one of the present generation of executive coaches who combine a business consultancy background with psychotherapy training and practice. In making the argument for coaches to possess psychological mindedness as well as business awareness and coaching skill he makes the point that 'it is quite common to encounter coaches who have a particular strength in one or two competencies but a weakness in another, and this creates lopsidedness in their coaching style.' He goes on to make the important point that coaches with a strong psychological background but who lack corporate knowledge and awareness tend to turn coaching into therapy. Conversely coaches from a corporate background who lack psychological mindedness may fail to engage with personal issues and focus too heavily on skills acquisition and problem solving.

It can be a difficult challenge for some coaches to stand back from their own experiencing to notice more of their internal processes and to suspend judgement about the other person's experience. Instead the tendency can be to get hooked by the client's story or issues and jump in with premature solutions in a desire to be helpful and move things on.

Later you might recognise this, perhaps when you reflect on the situation in supervision. You may then conclude that you became overinvolved, lost perspective or ran out of ideas as to how to proceed. To alleviate your own anxiety or discomfort you prematurely closed down the exploration of the issue by the client through offering practical suggestions. The outcome of this may be that you prevented your client from going where its was necessary to go.

The positive starts when you gain some perspective on these dynamics and become aware of how consciously or unconsciously you as the coach may affect the session. That recognition and acknowledgement can be the beginning of some very important personal development, which not only benefits you in your professional work but also in your personal life. A common limiting factor that I witness on a regular basis is the coach-in-training who is not comfortable with emotions being expressed. One coach put it this way: 'I'm OK with anger and frustration probably because they are the feelings I'm most able to express. But when it comes to hurt, sadness and grief I withdraw into myself and then try to move them away. It's because I don't allow these feelings in myself.'

This awareness on the part of the coach left her with questions for both her work and her wider life: – 'Do I want to address this? Am I ready to address it?' In the event, she did, and with profound effects for both areas of her life.

The underpinning components of psychological competence

The point is that self-awareness and awareness of others, often referred to as social awareness, are the fundamentals of psychological mindedness and that these capacities are the underpinning components of psychological competence for executive coaches.

There are a number of implications arising from this for the training of executive coaches as it suggests that *the personal development of the coach is every bit as important as theory and skill development*. Arguably there is no meaningful distinction between personal and professional development.

It also begs the question of whether psychological-mindedness can be developed and, if so, by what means. Having spent most of my working life in the business of developing psychological mindedness both in myself and others I have little doubt that it can, but it is usually a challenging process. It involves opening up, noticing more and being in the here and now more than we often are. It also entails a more questioning approach to life and a proactive engagement with others. It invariably involves risk, effort and discipline as you grapple to make more sense of your own experience and others' experiences. It can also be immensely satisfying and rewarding when you break through to some profound understandings and connections with others.

Developing psychological mindedness

When I picture individuals who have worked to develop their psychological mindedness I see people who are more obviously in touch with their inner experience and their interest in other people, and who allow themselves to follow their curiosity. They often ask more questions and probe that bit further. Their feedback to others has more depth, richness and impact. They are constantly seeking to understand what is really going on, not just what appears to be happening.

Opening up is also a fundamental aspect of the process. What this means in essence is to open your ears and eyes to hear and see more. Most of us miss a great deal of what goes on around us. It also means opening yourself to your own inner world: what you are aware of, thinking about, feeling and saying to yourself. But, as Lee (2003) points out, it is also about a growing self-knowledge that enables us to 'notice the preferences, biases, and blind spots that underpin our behaviour.' It's about recognising the patterns in our own and other people's behaviour – patterns of self-doubt, submission or aggression, the need to be liked, to withdraw or to be the centre of things.

All of this takes place in the here and now. Awareness is always present time. You can worry about or anticipate the future, you can reminisce about the past, but you are always doing these things in the present moment. Learning to 'be here now' is often a fundamental aspect of people's growth and development. When we are in the here and now we tend to make more meaningful contact with our environment, which is essential for personal satisfaction, relationship building and effective, appropriate action.

The personal development of the coach

There are several means to achieve this opening-up, here-and-now, more connected way of being. Most involve experientially focused work, which enhances self and social awareness. The most obvious of these are counselling and therapy either in a one-one or group context. Yoga, t'ai chi, meditation and a whole range of spiritually focused activities also provide routes to greater self-knowledge and deeper connectedness to self.

For the coach it is also useful to supplement any personally focused activities with development opportunities in the group context. This is because the purpose of personal development work is not simply to understand oneself better and act in a more self-aware manner. It is also to understand and appreciate others, to be able to connect with them and to respond appropriately.

Some of the most powerful vehicles for awareness raising in the group situation have been the experiential groups' derivative of the T-group and encounter group movement. Although these had their heyday in the 1950s to 1970s there has been a continuation and development of these methods ever since in the form of unstructured groups, awareness-raising groups, personal development groups and so on. They have varied in leadership style and purpose but the great value of all of these groups has been that they provide people with a live laboratory to learn more about self and 'other'. The common factor, whatever the preferred methodology, is the feedback-rich nature of these groups. You find out more about how you are seen and are prompted and encouraged to reveal more about yourself. In the process, many relevant coaching skills are learned and fine tuned, such as active listening, questioning, demonstrating understanding, and expressing empathy. The ability to give feedback in a skilled way is also learned as is the capacity to receive feedback in a non-defensive manner. In essence these groups are EI-learning laboratories.

The observing self

Casement (1985) makes the important distinction between the 'observing self' and the 'experiencing self'. This refers to our ability to look objectively at our thoughts, feelings and behaviours as well as experience them from the inside. Personal development work enables us to develop our 'observing self' and our capacity to be in 'Object' mode. This is a vital aspect of coach development because it is what psychological mindedness is founded on – an ability to notice your own experiencing and stand apart from it to observe and reflect on it.

This is particularly relevant for the coaching conversation. As a coach you need to be fully present, listening to the story yet at the same time stepping back to notice patterns and connections, some of which may be to do with your client's typical styles of relating and also those that stand out in the relationship between you.

This capability is also important because it allows the possibility of using self as instrument of change. This is where you tap into your own experience of being with the client and use internal data selectively as a source of intervention.

The ultimate purpose of personal development work is to be more tuned-in both cognitively and emotionally – tuned into your self, other people and the relationship between. It is that connectedness that enables rapport to develop, trust to be built and intelligent interventions to be made. It is the foundation of the psychological approach to coaching and is every bit as important as good theoretical understanding and a wide ranging coaching skill-set.

Further reflections on psychological mindedness

Over the years I have worked with people from a host of professional backgrounds and found high and low levels of psychological-mindedness across the piece. I have learned not to make assumptions about which occupational types score lowest or highest in psychological mindedness. For example, I have been fortunate to work with some outstanding soccer coaches from a Premiership football club who constantly seek to understand their own performance and that of their players in psychological terms. I have worked with scientists, engineers, financial accountants, investment bankers and police officers who are fascinated by the psychological meanings behind events. As one might expect, there have been many more from occupational psychology, counselling, HR, consultancy, training and OD who have displayed high levels of psychological mindedness.

There have also been a great many, including those from the coaching, HR and consultancy professions, who have manifested worryingly low levels of self- and social awareness despite having an apparent grasp of psychological theory and applications. Psychological training in an academic sense does not necessarily generate psychological mindedness as it may hardly touch on the awareness development of the student.

Some near-future issues

In the near future I believe we will see greater attention to the psychological development of the coach as a response to the growing awareness and acceptance in the field that psychological mindedness is one of the key higher level proficiencies of executive coaching. Beyond that there will be another set of questions that requires examination. What constitutes psychological competence? Does the coach, for example, require a good working knowledge of theories of personal change and how adults learn? Do coaches need an appreciation of one or more schools of psychology and, if so, which are the most applicable for coaches? Does the coach need a high level of psychological insight and an array of psychological skills and techniques? Is it necessary to be trained and competent in psychometric profiling and assessment instruments? Do we expect executive coaches to be able to provide a psychological 'holding environment' when their executive clients meet a crisis in their lives such as career derailment? And, back to the personal development of the coach, will we see guidelines on personal development emerge? Will coaches-in-training be required, as counselling trainees are, to be on the receiving end of coaching for a specified number of hours? And, perhaps most important of all, who will say so anyway? Will coaching arrive at a point where there is an authoritative professional body that sets such expectations and has the means to monitor them?

My own view is that psychological mindedness, and particularly a high level of self- and social awareness, stands as a baseline proficiency for executive coaching and is part of a wider group that constitutes psychological competence. That wider group includes theories of how people change and why they so often don't, schools of psychological thought and psychological insight. Psychological skills in the facilitation of behavioural change are also important. These and other similar issues are the subject of the next chapter.

10 The desirable proficiencies of psychologically oriented coaching

If psychological mindedness is the foundation stone of psychological competence for coaching then what are the additional conceptual understandings and practical skills that create the full structure? This chapter attempts to answer that question by setting out a framework of desirable proficiencies for psychologically oriented coaching. First, however, I want to clarify how I have arrived at them. The process has involved the following:

- Consultation with psychologically oriented coaches based around the question, 'What do you regard as the key aspects of psychological competence for coaches?'
- Key findings from the European Mentoring and Coaching Council (EMCC) research into coaching competencies.
- Researching the consulting psychology literature where the issue of psychological competencies for coaching is examined.
- My own experience as an executive coach and trainer of coaches in the psychological dimensions to coaching.

It is obvious that a psychologically oriented coaching approach requires a good level of psychological competence from the coach. The more difficult questions are to do with what level and how coaches are to develop it. If we believe that working with the psychological dimensions to coaching issues requires the very highest level of training and experience we may conclude that only clinically trained psychologists are fit to practise this work. This view has been expressed by a number of coaching writers, in the main psychologists (Berglas, 2002; Sperry, 2004).

One would expect a trained psychologist to possess some or even most of the vital proficiencies to work in more psychologically focused executive coaching. Occupational psychologists, for example, will have far more appreciation and relevant training in assessment processes involving the use of psychometric instruments and in some cases are the only people professionally endorsed to administer certain tests. Some may also be trained in behavioural tools and techniques.

Occupational psychology training, however, does not equip the practitioner with the capacity to diagnose pathology or clinical conditions in clients – a proficiency only likely to be found in clinically trained psychologists, psychiatrists or highly qualified psychotherapists.

It would be unrealistic to expect that many executive coaches will have any more than a rudimentary knowledge about complex psychological makeups. What is required is to equip people better and to alert them to sound professional practice so that they work within their genuine competence whilst simultaneously growing it.

My own general position, then, is this. Whilst senior practitioners in the field are absolutely right to sound the warning bells about undertrained coaches delving into areas best left to more advanced practitioners, the vast majority of executives and managers who become clients of coaches do not fall into the serious psychological problems category. The very nature of coaching means that, by and large, executive coaches work with relatively healthy individuals. Their issues are more to do with widening their repertoires of behaviour, controlling their emotional responses, developing their EI, getting closure around unfinished issues, cultivating leadership presence and, for some, finding out what they really want from the rest of their lives. These contain a psychological dimension but do not constitute disturbance. For the most part they are simply aspects of the human condition and issues that most people have to grapple with.

Secondly, you will usually know when you are starting to get out of your depth. Your trainers should help you develop your gut instincts, which tell you to back off on those occasions when your personal alarm bells are ringing. A practical guideline is to always work within your level of competence and take complex psychological issues to your supervisor to gain a more experienced perspective.

My main concern is more to do with novice coaches rushing off too quickly with new-found tools and techniques gained on short courses or from self-development books and coaching manuals. This is where more harm gets done and it is for this very reason that there are very few 'how-to-do-it exercises' in this book. I strongly believe that psychologically oriented processes need to be learned in a properly managed training environment.

The more self-developed you are as a coach the less likely you are to do this as you will appreciate the potency of some of these methods and understand the importance of learning your trade carefully over time. You will also recognise the need to devote as much time, energy and attention to your own self-development as you do to theory and skill development. The most dangerous coaches are those who either don't appreciate the need for self-development or, worse still, believe they are much further down the line than they really are.

With these health warnings in mind, it is equally important to remember that most coaches and coaches-in-training take these issues very seriously indeed. They are often exemplary in their commitment to good professional practice and anxious to take their training and development at the right pace to ensure learning is embedded before practising on real people.

The list of proficiencies in Table 10.1 is offered for those coaches whose work already takes a stronger psychological orientation and to those coaches aspiring to work at greater depth. Inevitably, any list will be less than exhaustive. That being said, I believe it is sufficiently comprehensive to inform advanced training and development programmes which take a more psychological approach to coaching.

Table 10.1. Desirable proficiencies for psychologically oriented coaching

Broader category	Example competencies
1 Conceptual understanding (theory)	1 Has an appreciation of one or more schools of psychology – e.g. person centred, cognitive, behavioural, psychodynamic, Gestalt, etc. 2 Understands theories of change 3 Has an appreciation of psychological concepts 4 Understands the thinking, feeling, behaviour connection 5 Has an understanding of behavioural change models and techniques
2 Assessment processes	6 Is familiar with a broad range of assessment tools and techniques 7 Is trained/competent to deliver at least one, e.g. psychometric, EI or 360-degree feedback 8 Has integrated assessment processes into own coaching practice
3 Psychological mindedness	9 Reflects on the causes and meanings behind own and other people's thoughts, feelings and behaviour 10 Seeks to recognise the links between current issues and past events
4 Self-awareness	11 Is aware of own inner world – body sensations, self-talk, mood, optimism/pessimism, etc. 12 Understands own emotions 13 Has understanding of own drivers and motivations
5 Social awareness	14 Can sense other people's emotions 15 Actively seeks to understand others' perspectives, concerns and feelings 16 Suspends judgement about the others' thoughts, feelings and behaviour 17 Demonstrates accurate understanding of others' emotions 18 Conveys empathy in a sensitive manner

6 Self-management	19 Can separate own feelings from those of the client 20 Ensures that own beliefs, values and opinions do not adversely affect the coaching process 21 Keeps own difficult emotions and impulses under control
7 Relationship skills	22 Can establish rapport with a wide range of people 23 Can provide the conditions for effective helping relationships: non-judgemental stance, acceptance, empathy, genuineness and warmth 24 Can manage the complexities of the triangular relationship common to corporate coaching
8 Psychological understandings and insight	25 Recognises when unfinished situations in clients may be affecting their current performance 26 Identifies patterns, themes and issues that may be being reenacted from the past 27 Distinguishes feelings, thoughts and reactions evoked by others from those deriving from self 28 Can identify psychological complexity 29 Has some awareness of pathology 30 Can differentiate between coaching and therapeutic issues 31 Identifies issues and material to bring to supervision
9 Psychological skills	32 Can facilitate heightened awareness 33 Creates a safe environment where client can explore issues and experiment with new thinking and behaviour 34 Helps the client understand and manage his/her emotions more effectively 35 Can provide effective support and challenge 36 Can facilitate emotional expression appropriately 37 Can use the here and now moment as a source of direct learning 38 Uses self effectively – own internal data as a source of intervention
10 Holding environment	39 Can support client effectively in 'critical' situations that are emotionally intense 40 Can maintain emotional balance when things are emotionally charged and/or get complex
11 Professionalism	41 Understands the importance of self-development as part of the process of achieving competence 42 Understands and adheres to the highest standard of professional practice 43 Works to level of competence and does not misrepresent own expertise 44 Engages in one-one, group or peer supervision 45 Is committed to continuing professional development (CPD)

More detail may be useful on some of the example competencies (right-hand column) in order to get hold of the broader categories (left-hand column). I won't attempt to cover all of them; instead I'll focus on just a few that may not be immediately obvious.

Possessing a theory of change

The first category, conceptual understanding, is particularly important. Although most coaches recognise that they are in the change business, many cannot articulate how they understand change takes place, and why so often it doesn't. Having a theory of change is indispensable to psychologically oriented coaching.

Probably the best known and most scientifically validated change model is the Prochaska stages of change model set out in a number of research articles and books cowritten with Norcross, DiClemente and Velicer, dating back as far as 1979. This emerging body of work has influenced such diverse activities as health promotion campaigns, addiction treatment, psychotherapy practice, leadership programmes and mainstream education. It proposes that change is a process that unfolds over time and involves a progression through a number of stages, namely: precontemplation, contemplation, preparation, action, maintenance and termination. These are supported by a number of change processes such as awareness raising, reevaluation of self, and experimentation with new behaviours. Other key change factors such as decisional balance, the cost-benefit analysis of change, and self-efficacy are also prominent in this theory. Given the impact of this work it is important to examine it in more detail.

Prochaska's stages of change

Pre-contemplation is characterised by the following:

- The clients concerned are not intending to change or take action in the near future (the next 6 months).
- They may be uninformed or underinformed about the consequences and effects of their behaviour.
- They may have tried to change previously but were unsuccessful (and maybe demoralised).
- They may be in denial or defensive.

According to Prochaska, people in the pre-contemplation stage 'underestimate the benefits of changing and overestimate the costs'.

Contemplation is where individuals intend to change within the next 6 months and where the following typically apply:

- They are more aware of the advantages of changing but are also acutely conscious of the disadvantages.
- The perceived costs of change can increase at this stage.
- This can produce a profound ambivalence.

This *cost/benefit analysis of change*, so intrinsic to the process, is what leads to the critical factor of *decisional balance* – where the scales tip in favour of one course of action (or inaction).

The *preparation* stage is reached when a person intends to take action in the next month and is beginning to scan the environment for the information, practical assistance and emotional support required to succeed. It might be the time when as a coach you are first approached by a prospective client.

The *action* stage is when the person has genuinely engaged with the 'programme' and is taking actions identified to address targeted behaviours. It is characterised by the following:

- The individual has made specific, overt modifications.
- Improvement is observable and measurable.
- The benefits of change are beginning to appear.

Maintenance is the stage where people are aware of the dangers of relapsing into old behaviours yet are simultaneously becoming more confident that they can hold onto their hard-won gains. This is a critical yet often underestimated stage of the change process.

One of the most common reasons for relapse is that people invariably think that their change effort will require a few weeks or months at the most and ease up on both their resolve and conscious actions too early. Using clients' own reports, Prochaska suggests that the maintenance phase may require anything from 6 months to 5 years.

The sixth and final stage is defined as *termination*. This applies more obviously when people are giving up a habit or an unhealthy pattern of coping and have reached the point when they experience a rock solid belief that they will not return to it. This level of self-efficacy is relatively low according to Prochaska's studies and, as he points out, 'for many people the best that can be accomplished is a life-time of maintenance'. This figure has to be seen in the context of studies on clinical populations where clients were changing high habit-strength behaviours such as problem drinking and chronic addiction to smoking.

Change processes

In addition to these six stages of change Prochaska and his research colleagues identified nine processes of change that need to be matched to the relevant stage:

- Increased awareness – recognition of the issue(s). This particularly applies at the precontemplation and contemplation stages.
- Emotional awareness – experiencing and expressing feelings about the issue(s). Again, especially relevant at the first two stages.
- Consideration of the impact of behaviour on others. Again, stages one and two.
- Reevaluation of self in relation to feelings about the issue[s]. 'Am I the person I thought I was?' 'What sort of person do I want to be?' This process of change can propel the individual from contemplation to preparation.
- A belief that one can change and a commitment to act. This may be the driving force to move from preparation to action.
- Experimentation with new behaviours and responses – learning new and more productive ways to achieve goals. This change process together with the remaining three all fit both the action and maintenance stages.
- Incentives and rewards for changes, particularly self-reinforced ones.
- Avoidance of triggers in the environment for old behaviour.
- Development of support networks including the coach, friends, family and colleagues

Implications for the coach

Prochaska's work offers some invaluable learning points about coaching for behavioural change. It provides illuminating insights into how change takes place and why so often it doesn't. These are some of the points which I believe are especially relevant to coaches:

- The model reinforces the importance of identifying the stage your clients are at in their change process. This may seem obvious but I would suggest that coaches often mistakenly treat their clients as if they are in the preparation or action stage when they are actually in the precontemplation or contemplation stages. This places the coach and the client on different pages of the book. What invariably follows is confusion and disappointment as the clients fail to live up to the coach's expectations.
- This body of research yet again emphasises the importance of raising awareness as a crucial aspect of the change process. It also underpins another central principle of coaching – that a person must choose to commit to learning and change. The power of that decision should not be underestimated.
- The reevaluation of self in the light of new data about oneself requires of the client a deeper psychological process and reaffirms the

need for the coach to be psychologically skilled and able to work with people in vulnerable states.

- This research provides a reminder of just how important a role the environment plays in the change process either reinforcing or undermining success. This underlines the need for the coach to take a systems perspective in personal change work.

- Prochaska's studies confirm that change requires longer than people often think. It can therefore be important to discuss realistic time-frames for change with clients. It also suggests that we need to pay fuller attention to the maintenance stage of change. In organisational life, where things move on quickly and agendas change, maintenance is often neglected. This may account for why so many change initiatives fall away.

- Finally, this work lends support to the view that ultimately coaching is about promoting self-change and that this may indeed be your most significant contribution as a coach.

Given the scope of this change theory it isn't possible to cover all its major propositions here. I therefore recommend that you explore the source material in depth. Having a strong appreciation of a credible theory of change is an indispensable part of any coach's toolkit.

Complex psychological makeups

The issue of psychological complexity and pathology also warrants further attention. These terms relate to more pronounced psychological problems such as depression, severe anxiety, addiction, narcissism and personality disorders.

These conditions do exist in organisational life and it has to be recognised that all coaches working with executives over a significant period of time will sooner or later find themselves working with someone with pronounced psychological problems of this kind. Sometimes the problem will reveal itself through the effects the executives concerned are having on their immediate colleagues. There will usually be serious disquiet and concern about this individual, which often gets communicated to the coach. Another sign may be the level of stress colleagues are experiencing or the fact that illness rates are unusually high.

Coaches coming from senior management or HR backgrounds themselves will usually have first-hand experience of complex psychological scenarios and may quickly tune into the tell-tale signs of high anxiety and withdrawal. In these situations it is very important that, as a coach, you recognise the professional risks, dangers and pitfalls of coaching executives who have significant psychological problems. If things go wrong then you can find yourself with a career-threatening adversary. Your intention may only have been to support the individual, not change or therapise him. However, if individuals are unstable they may lash out in any direction including yours. Faced with a situation of this kind it is essential that you use your professional supervision to explore the coaching dynamic and gain personal support.

The holding environment

One final competence category that may need further definition is the concept of the *holding environment*. This concept derives from psychotherapy and refers to an aspect of the helping relationship that is about providing a safe enough, strong enough space to contain the stresses in the situation. This most often comes into play when clients experience a crisis in their life. In corporate coaching this may derive from the person's private life but is most likely to take the shape of career derailment. Given the prevalence of this phenomenon it is just a question of time before a client arrives at a coaching session with the bad news. At this point it is important to increase the level of active support and create a stronger container. On occasions it may catch you off guard. It may happen on one of your off days yet you still have to find that bit more for your client and stay emotionally balanced in the midst of powerfully charged feelings. This is a time for thinking on your feet and also feeling on your feet.

Some of the specific examples I've chosen to focus on here such as complex psychological problems and career derailment may worry you if you are new to coaching. 'Is this what I'm going to be confronted by?' may be a question going through your mind. The good news is that these are not everyday coaching themes. As I have already stressed, they are more the exception than the norm. However we must acknowledge that they are part and parcel of executive coaching and the more equipped the coach is to identify them and then work appropriately the better.

Developing these proficiencies

How, then, can you develop these proficiencies if you wish to make this journey? Do you need to go off and train as a clinical or occupational psychologist? Should you sign up for a diploma programme in counselling or therapy? Will attendance on some weekend workshops supplemented by some focused reading do the job? Will accreditation courses to deliver psychometric processes or a training to assess emotional intelligence be enough?

At present many coaches, both experienced and novice, are searching around to find developmental experiences to fill gaps of which they are acutely aware in their knowledge, practice and personal development. The proficiencies outlined in this chapter can take a lifetime to develop to a high level. There is no quick fix or wonder course that can equip people to work professionally in the psychological domain of coaching. Nor should there be. The journey to deeper self-knowledge and psychological competence takes a long time. Slowing down and savouring the journey is probably the wisest and ultimately most satisfying approach.

In the next chapter I look at the whole question of developing as a coach across all the higher level competency categories. As part of this exploration I will present a number of vehicles through which you might develop your psychological competency for coaching and address your own personal and professional development issues.

11 Developing as a coach

Introduction

As a provider of advanced coach training I am regularly contacted by new and experienced coaches alike who are looking for appropriate coaching development for themselves. They often use the word 'minefield' to describe what they perceive to be the coach training marketplace. Those who have taken their research seriously report their utter confusion and frustration with what appears to be an anarchic state of affairs. There are some providers claiming to train world-class coaches in 3 to 5 days, others suggest that postgraduate programmes of one to three years are the real thing, and everything else in between. Some programmes are workshop based. Others are delivered as distance-learning packages through electronic communication. The structure, content and approach of programmes vary enormously as does the background of those delivering them, ranging from internationally known academics to management development trainers.

This, of course, is one of the products of an unregulated field with, as yet, no commonly agreed professional competency frameworks, standards, theory or positions on good practice. The field is rapidly moving towards this but still has some way to go. In the meantime those looking for bona fide coach training will continue to go round the same maze.

There are four aspects to a training and development framework for professional coaching:

1   Theoretical development
2   Practice/skill development
3   Personal development
4   Professional development

1 Theoretical development

Having spent many years training and developing coaches and consultants it is crystal clear that people have different reactions to theory. Some love it and eagerly arrive at training sessions hoping to glean that new insight or connection. Others see it as a necessary evil and give far greater weight to practice and skill development. Coach trainers, however, cannot afford to dilute the theoretical side of coach development if coaching is to present itself to the world as a valid professional activity. Good practice needs to be founded on solid thinking as well as proven training methods.

So where does coaching look for its theory? In the past the main sources have been psychology – organisational and consulting psychology on the one hand and sports psychology on the other. More recently it has borrowed concepts from psychotherapy and counselling. Other important sources have been theories of adult learning, organisational development, and management and leadership theory. Ideas and concepts emerging from personal success literature, the self-help books on how to change your life in easy steps, have also found their way into coaching, particularly life coaching.

Coaching theory could be said to be an amalgam of thinking from other disciplines. But does coaching have any of its own? I believe it does and that we are likely to see a growing body of theory emerging from the coaching field as it matures. Historically, Gallwey's inner and outer game coaching is a prime example of landmark thinking that has had a significant influence on the way coaching is understood and practised.

Best fit psychological framework?

The question of whether one particular psychological framework is the best fit for coaching already occupies the minds of a number of practitioners and academics, and coaching approaches are emerging based on many of the most recognised schools such as psychodynamic, cognitive behavioural, Gestalt and constructive-developmental psychology. If coaching reflects a similar trend to psychotherapy and counselling then it is likely that a strong claim will be made that cognitive-behavioural psychology is the psychology of preference for coaching. This would not be to everyone's liking, nor would everyone agree with it, and we can expect to hear practitioners from psychodynamic, person-centred, Gestalt and constructive-developmental backgrounds all making their own powerful cases.

The arguments will increasingly be framed in academic terms and scientific research will be used to justify the propositions being made. This will inevitably produce an uneven playing field as some of the psychological frameworks mentioned above have been slow or even reluctant to investigate their own outcomes using traditional academic methods. They therefore have little to offer up when the academic debates occupy centre stage.

However I think there is a completely different question that precedes the schoolism arguments. That question relates to the critical factors outlined in Part 1 concerning coaching principles, process, the coach's competence, the relationship and the client. It is quite possible that these will turn out to be every bit as important to successful coaching outcomes as the specific model, psychological or not, the coach works from.

In time we will have research to tell us, but in the meantime I think a useful way of viewing psychological frameworks is that the coach is probably better off with one than without one. Secondly, your practice is likely to improve if you become genuinely knowledgeable and skilled in that framework. This is not, however, an argument for a 'one-framework-only' approach. Many coaches are eclectic and prefer to draw on concepts from several psychological models.

The coach-training business may become increasingly differentiated in the future, with providers specialising in programmes with a psychodynamic, Gestalt or cognitive-behavioural focus. There would be some value in this but personally I hope that we see a more integrative approach where coaches-in-training are exposed to ideas and concepts from a wide range of psychological traditions. A move to a more prescriptive situation could stifle creativity and polarise the field.

2 Practice/skill development

Advanced coach training programmes and particularly those offering post-graduate qualifications have been in increasing demand during the past few years. Some delegates on these programmes are more academically minded and take easily to the theoretical as well as the skill development sides of the course. Others are perfectly capable of taking on the reading and assignments but are hampered by a confidence issue around academic work, feel apprehensive about it, and sometimes perform less well.

Imagine then if these masters, diploma and certificate programmes were to offer their awards purely on the basis of passing written assignments. We would then see academically bright people graduating from these courses to proclaim themselves qualified coaches based only on the ability to deliver on the theoretical aspect to coaching. Their ability to coach may be poor and yet they would legitimately be able to practise and claim a 'professional' credibility on the back of a reputable university award.

Clearly this is a worrying aspect of coach training as coaching is not simply an academic subject. Indeed, on the contrary, it is a highly practical activity requiring a wide range of skill-sets. A conceptual understanding of transference does not imply that the coach can recognise and work with it in a complex coaching relationship. A strong theoretical interest in the subject of EI does not guarantee that the coach has a high degree of self-awareness and a deep capacity to empathise with others.

For these reasons it is essential that a credible coach-training process addresses skill development (and personal development in the case of EI) as well as theoretical development. How that is achieved will vary with different programmes but this is a fundamental aspect of coach development. My own view is that skill development needs to be based around two methodologies. The first is the tried-and-tested practice/feedback model of learning and the second is professionally supervised practice.

The practice/feedback model has been applied in both counselling/ therapy and process consultancy training for several decades throughout the world. It works like this: course delegates work in small groups of three or four supported by a tutor. Each group member rotates around the roles of coach, client and observer so that everyone gets to practise their coaching in a live situation working on genuine issues and gaining feedback from the observer(s) and tutor. The sessions can be videoed and shown later as a supplementary method of audio/visual feedback. The value of the learning depends on the quality of feedback from the course tutor and the observer(s). In reality this tends to be high, particularly on postgraduate programmes, which attract experienced, highly competent individuals. Typically, practising coaches get to understand more clearly what they are currently doing well and where their learning edge is. They then use this feedback to inform their subsequent practice sessions.

Supervised practice is another excellent method of skill development. Whether the coach is experienced or is in the early stages of training it is important to have a place to explore one's work with a fellow practitioner in a supervision context. In a training programme it can be reassuring and helpful for course members to receive supervision on the coaching practice they undertake between workshops. It also provides a quality-control mechanism for the client. If the supervision is provided in a group situation then each member potentially learns something of significant value from witnessing others receiving their supervision. It also gets them into the regular experience of a practice that they will hopefully continue on an ongoing basis following their training.

3 Personal development

When prospective coaching students do their initial research to find a suitable advanced programme they tend to look for evidence of theoretical rigour balanced with opportunities to practise. Some also check whether there is an accent on personal development and, if so, how it is addressed. They recognise that effective coach training requires more than a focus on tools, techniques and models.

There are many vehicles through which coaches can focus on their own personal development and gain greater self-awareness, insight and knowledge. Some of these activities can be undertaken in parallel and some may already be structured into an advanced coach training programme. They are:

1   Coaching psychology programmes
2   Counselling/psychology training
3   Being coached
4   Personal therapy/counselling
5   Experiential workshops
6   Ongoing groups
7   Supervision
8   Personal study/reading

Options for self-development

Coaching psychology programmes are new to the coaching field but can be expected to proliferate in the coming years. It is common for coaches to reach a point when they ask themselves whether they need to undertake a longer programme of development in psychology, psychotherapy or counselling. Some do and find it of great value to them in their coaching. It may take them off in the direction of becoming a professional therapist, counsellor or psychologist. Most, of course, don't because of the time, commitment and cost. A full psychological training will always provide knowledge and skills that will enhance coaching effectiveness, but for many coaches it will be a step too far.

The issue of being coached raises the interesting point that many practising coaches appear to have little personal experience of being on the receiving end of coaching unless they have undertaken training that uses the practice/feedback model or where a course requirement stipulated a certain number of hours to be coached.

For many, therapy still has an unfavourable association with it: it suggests you are not functioning well enough – a theme that doesn't always sit well in coaching. For that reason many trainee coaches baulk at the idea of going into therapy themselves. Yet therapy remains one of the most powerful processes available to people to go deeper into their personal development issues and, for some, may be the only way they will ever truly understand and make progress on some of their most persistent, intractable personal patterns.

Therapy and counselling training typically involve being in the client seat as part of the overall development process. Though this can be fairly minimal, around 40 hours, it nevertheless provides the trainee counsellor or psychologist with a taste of what it means to be in that vulnerable place while also providing an opportunity to address more deep-seated issues. Some coach trainings are following suit in that they are building into their structures that course members must be on the receiving end of coaching for precisely the same reasons.

Attending workshops and ongoing experiential groups can also be an enormously helpful route to self-development. The group environment offers a feedback-rich learning context where coaches can extend their self- and social awareness, experiment with new behaviours and discover more about their impact and presence. Short courses and workshops in psychological frameworks such as psychosynthesis and Gestalt will typically combine content-specific learning with important personal growth opportunities.

Perhaps the most underestimated vehicle and the most difficult to find is the ongoing experiential group. Older readers may recall the T-groups, encounter groups and consciousness-raising groups of the 1960s and 1970s, which for some was their original learning ground for psychologically focused work. Whilst derivatives of these do exist they are far fewer and harder to locate. This kind of ongoing group is a special place and relationships achieve great depth. For these reasons they can be a central part of a coach's self-development journey.

Any list of methods to develop oneself must include reading and private study. There is now a massive number of self-development manuals and success literature, which can open people up to new, helpful and sometimes inspirational concepts and ideas. As part of a wider range of development activities they have an important place and contribution. On their own they will not always be enough. The whole premise of coaching and any helping activity is that the process of externalising the issue to another human being, or several in the case of groupwork, provides that missing ingredient which facilitates change and development. Simply reading self-development books on one's own may expand our consciousness but may be too inward a process on its own.

Developing as a coach, particularly if you work more psychologically, requires a commitment to your own personal development and addressing, in a deeper way, your own personal issues. Initially, students don't always make the connection between learning how to coach and looking into themselves. They have come to a coaching programme to learn some tools and techniques to 'do to' other people – and to get a professional ticket. By the end of the process they typically regard the awareness development aspect of their training as *the* most important part. They also appreciate the critical importance of EI as a key psychological competency of the coach.

4 Professional development

Although executive coaching cannot yet be described as a profession it is nevertheless essential that those calling themselves coaches conduct themselves in a professional manner. Coach training programmes and especially those preparing executive coaches must therefore pay strong attention to the professional development agenda.

Practitioners coming into coaching from psychological and therapeutic backgrounds will typically be well schooled in these issues and be conscious of appropriate professional boundaries. Those from corporate and sporting backgrounds may be used to quite different working boundaries. A coach from a therapeutic background, for example, would have serious misgivings about conducting a coaching session in a busy hotel reception area in case deeper issues arise that require a stronger holding environment. A coach from a management or HR background may think nothing of it. It is common to hear coaches describe a coaching session held over dinner with a bottle of wine in a restaurant.

At present the coaching field is not yet mature enough to have come to grips with all of these scenarios. There is a wide range of views about what constitutes good practice and those viewpoints largely reflect the professional background of the coach. Having said that the field has begun to grapple with the issues and a number of aspiring professional bodies and associations such as the European Mentoring and Coaching Council (EMCC), the Association for Coaching (AC), the Association for Professional Coaches and Supervisors (APECS), and the International Coaching Federation (ICF), have published codes of ethics, and guidelines for good practice. These organisations are growing in membership and influence and contain an increasing number of coaches who have an exemplary commitment to the highest standards of professional practice.

Coaching supervision

It is likely that coaching bodies will look to three main vehicles for raising standards of coaching practice now and in the future: structured training and development programmes, accreditation processes for practitioners and coach training providers, and supervision.

Supervision is not a new concept. It has been practised in social work, psychotherapy and counselling, and clinical psychology for decades. Its role in apprenticeship and sound management goes back even further. Professional supervision, as opposed to management supervision, is nevertheless fairly new in the coaching field. If you trace the references to supervision in the best known coaching texts you will barely find anything before the millennium. Hardly any of the standard texts up to that point even discuss it. That situation is now changing rapidly and there are a growing number of professional coaches and mentors who regard supervision as essential to good practice. Many of these come from psychological and therapeutic backgrounds or have been recently influenced to see the virtue of supervision.

So what does coaching supervision look like? Firstly, it is time and place to reflect on ones work either with a senior colleague, in a led group, or with a number of peers. The purpose of that reflection is to make greater sense of difficult and complex work assignments and to gain more clarity going forward. Secondly, it is an opportunity to receive support, both practical, in the form of ideas and suggestions, and emotional, in the sense of sharing issues and when appropriate receiving reassurance. Thirdly, supervision can be a place for ongoing learning and professional development following earlier training.

Supervision for different stages

Those who have studied and written on the subject and those who have been in supervision during their careers tend to agree that supervision means different things at different stages of our careers. The newcomer to coaching, who may still be in training, will have different needs from an experienced executive coach who has been operating in the business for 10 or 20 years. The 'trainee' will perhaps require clearer guidance and closer attention to the anxieties often experienced in those early days. The seasoned coach will probably want a more equal, consultative relationship. The amount and frequency of supervision will also vary.

The key functions of supervision

One of the most influential writers on supervision has been Kadushin (1976) who defined three main functions: the educational development of the practitioner and the fulfilment of potential, the practical and psychological support to carry through the responsibilities of the role, and the promotion and maintenance of good standards of work and adherence to policies and good practice. This is the quality-assurance dimension to supervision. Proctor (1986) also has a similar view of the key functions of supervision although her terminology is different. She refers to the normative, formative and restorative aspects of supervision.

How supervision works

The process usually involves a presentation of a specific case or a set of issues that are concerning the coach, to acquire a deeper understanding of what is taking place for the client, in the relationship between the coach and client, and for the coach. This learning serves the purpose of addressing all three functions. Coaches develop deeper knowledge and wisdom about their work, are steered towards good practice and feel reassured and guided.

Other purposes of supervision have been outlined by Hawkins and Shohet (2001). It can focus on session content, strategies and interventions used by the coach and the nature of the supervisory relationship itself.

Examples of supervision issues

Throughout this book I have referred to a variety of supervision issues. Here are some further ones:

- Chemistry is an important aspect of the coaching relationship. A positive liking and an immediate empathy for your client will always feel better and give you that reassuring sense of looking forward to the work. However, this won't always be the case and your challenge as a coach may be to find out what it is that makes this client difficult for you. Exploring this in supervision can produce important insights and free you up to work more effectively with your current client and those with similar characteristics in the future.
- You may be struggling to find the balance between support and challenge in your work with your clients. Supervision may reveal a developmental issue in one or even both these areas. The supervisor might suggest that you undertake further personal development to understand and address the underlying issues.
- You might be feeling that your work with a particular client isn't progressing well and you are not clear why not. Talking this through in supervision can help you get unstuck.
- If you think that you might be working with someone with a more complex psychological makeup then it is essential to explore this with your supervisor to gain another perspective and the support required to undertake this work.
- Your client might be struggling with a profound dilemma about whether to 'whistle-blow' on a colleague or boss due to perceived financial irregularities. This kind of issue may be outside your experience as a coach and leave you apprehensive and uncertain. Discussing it with your supervisor can provide you with much-needed guidance and reassurance.
- You might be suffering a crisis of personal confidence in your work and be questioning whether you are cut out for executive coaching. Your supervision space will give you the opportunity to explore and better understand what is causing this and give you that support to keep going and ride it out.

Format for supervision

In practical terms supervision occurs in either one-one or group sessions. Typically the supervisor will be an experienced coach who has a good working knowledge of the supervision process, particularly when supervising trainee or novice coaches. Peer supervision is an increasingly popular mode due to a lack of supervisor availability and zero costs but in my view it should not be advocated for coaches in their early stage of development. Peers may be too inexperienced themselves to understand some of the complexities and will not be in a position to provide the community of practice function so important to consolidating good professional practice. As you become more experienced it is more appropriate to look at peer arrangements as an option.

Guidelines for supervision

Currently there are no nationally agreed guidelines as to the regularity of supervision. However the practice of supervision is strongly advocated by all the leading professional associations for coaching and mentoring.

Some coaching consultancies have prepared their own recommended formulas for the amount of supervision in relation to practice hours. These tend to vary from 1:8 to 1:15 hours supervision to practice. There is typically an implicit and sometimes explicit assumption that coaches-in-training or in their early career stages require the lower ratio.

Who can supervise?

This all assumes that there are supervisors out there ready and available to supervise. However this is not necessarily the case. The coaching field is still bottom-heavy in terms of experience. There is an ever-increasing number of newcomers and relatively few old hands. Experienced coaches are offering their services as supervisors but there is a need for more. This can make it difficult for coaches to find a supervisor.

Some coaches have found an answer to this by going to see counselling or therapy supervisors who are far more numerous at the present time than coaching supervisors. The advantage of this is that they are likely to be highly skilled and able to spot psychological dimensions within the coaching situation. The downside can be that they often lack corporate knowledge and may struggle to appreciate some of the context-specific issues.

As the coaching field continues to mature we will see an increasing number of short and longer courses to train coaches to become coaching supervisors. These are already appearing on the market and will result in a greater supply of supervisors in the medium and longer term.

The psychological debate

One of the issues occupying the minds of many senior coaches is how much psychological training and background is needed to operate as a supervisor. Those coaches who have come from psychology, counselling or therapy backgrounds tend to see this as absolutely essential. Typically these coaches recognise the psychological and emotional dimension to performance issues earlier and with greater clarity than their (psychologically) untrained counterparts. They may work to a different boundary and depth with their clients and therefore regard supervision as a psychological process too. Certainly some of the aspects of supervision mentioned earlier in Hawkins and Shohet (2001) would indicate a strong psychological competence required of the supervisor.

However, if you are one of the many coaches without a counselling/ therapy background you may regard it as unnecessary to be supervised by someone who has such a background. Your work may be more strategically rather than behaviourally focused and you may regard supervision more as a process of consultation.

For these reasons there is a need for different kinds of supervisors who can offer different perspectives. Strategic coaches may get most of what they need from their supervisors until the time comes when they are confronted by a client who has a complex psychological profile and may be experiencing problems. At this point they may be better advised to book some supervision sessions with a supervisor with a clinical background. In other words you may need to be able to draw on the services of more than one supervisor depending on the need at the time.

Whose interests does supervision serve?

Supervision serves your interests as a coach and also those of the client. The management function of the supervisor is about ensuring that, as a coach, you are working responsibly and ethically. However, good supervision is also about your educational and support needs. Skilled supervisors have the challenging job of keeping their focus on two agendas. If they simply look after the coach or adopt a trainer role and fail to address faulty practice issues then trouble may well lie ahead. Conversely, the supervisor who maintains a focus on practice issues without attending to the support and learning needs of their supervisee is not grasping a key aspect of the role. Acting as a supervisor is a demanding and sometimes complex, anxiety-provoking task. This is why it is helpful if supervisors are experienced practitioners in their own right, understand the nature of supervision, and have had first-hand experience of being supervised.

Professional supervision is now seen by many as a fundamental aspect of good practice as a coach and it may soon become one of the main methods of regulating the emerging profession.

PART 4

Supporting people through change – a Gestalt perspective

12 Creating the conditions for change

Introduction

If you are relatively new to Gestalt you probably associate it with Gestalt therapy, and up until recent decades this was by far its most common usage. In fact Gestalt therapy has been practised since the 1950s and you can find training institutes and Gestalt therapists all over the world. What is less well known is how Gestalt has been applied to one-one consultation (consultancy and coaching) in the organisational setting and to systems at other levels such as couples, families, groups (both small and large), workplace teams and communities.

The earliest use of Gestalt in the organisational context is attributed to Nevis and Wallen who began using Gestalt in management development programmes around 1960. Sensitivity training, as it was called then, used awareness-raising methods and techniques to assist managers in their personal development. This theme, the use of the Gestalt approach to facilitate self-development, runs through to this day although the original scope of sensitivity training is now the domain of EI development. The nature and objectives of this type of work nevertheless remain very similar.

Following his applications of Gestalt to management programmes Nevis combined with several others through the US-based Gestalt Institute of Cleveland to develop Gestalt theory and practice around organisational change and the consultancy process. Through their international training programmes they have influenced the practice of hundreds, perhaps thousands, of senior OD practitioners from all over the world in the applications of Gestalt to the organisational arena. Nevis's *Organisational Consulting: A Gestalt Approach* written in 1987 was a significant milestone along the way as it set out more clearly than ever before the key tenets of the Gestalt approach to consultancy and system change and development.

During the same period Sonia Nevis along with Joseph Zinker, applied Gestalt to work with couples and families. Their model, with its strong focus on relationship, has come to be known as the Cape Cod Model and takes a systemic approach. Practitioners and trainers from the Gestalt Institute of Cleveland and those they have trained and influenced, myself included, have taken the Gestalt approach through their organisation development practices into governmental agencies, corporate boardrooms and executive development programmes. The Gestalt method has been used as a primary underpinning theory and practice for executive coaching, team development, trainer and consultant development, and large group interventions.

The focus of this final section is to explore the application of Gestalt to executive coaching and discover what it has to offer coaches. Much of what you will find will be about the process of change and how to intervene more effectively as a change agent. These are fundamental issues to coaches as they provide a framework for practice. To cover them I will address a range of core ideas and concepts from Gestalt including the following:

- Fundamental propositions of Gestalt.
- How change takes place and the meaning of resistance.
- Awareness and change.
- The focus on the here and now.
- The Cycle of Experience.
- Working with unfinished business.
- The use of self as instrument of change.

But before all that, there is the awkward question of what this word 'Gestalt' means.

Gestalt defined

Whenever I begin work with a new group of coaches-in-training I ask them to brainstorm what they already know about Gestalt. It tends to be the least satisfying aspect of the day because Gestalt, a German word, does not easily translate into English. Different texts on Gestalt offer these translations: form, shape, pattern and configuration. This, in my experience, doesn't illuminate a great deal until we start to talk more about the notion of Gestalt as a whole, different from and more than the sum of its parts. Most people attach more meaning to this – yet it hardly passes the accessibility test.

Clarkson (2004) defines it as well as anyone when she says:

> The aim of the Gestalt approach is for a person to discover, explore and experience his or her own shape, pattern and wholeness. Analysis may be a part of the process, but the aim of Gestalt is the integration of all disparate parts. In this way people can let themselves become totally what they already are, and what they potentially can become.

Taking this definition you may see some immediate resonance with what coaching is about, particularly in the notions of being who we are and what we might become.

Fundamental propositions of Gestalt

At the heart of Gestalt lies a number of important propositions about the nature of human functioning and how change takes place. These also have much in common with the main principles underpinning coaching:

- That awareness leads to change.
- That the aim of the coach is to help clients to become more aware of their own process (their functioning).
- That this heightened awareness will produce a greater understanding of what is needed, what choices are open, and will ultimately produce more effective decision making and action.
- That the awareness-raising process produces greater personal ownership and responsibility.
- That our emerging, dominant needs organise our field of perception.
- That we perceive in wholes and seek to gain closure around issues.
- That we need to give meaning to our perceptions and experience.
- That learning occurs through the examination of here and now experience.

Many of these propositions may require no further explanation but there are some which might be unfamiliar. A classic Gestalt premise is that our *needs organise our field of perception*. I personally came across this idea in the early stages of my training at a time when my first son was just a few months old. At that time I would take him around our local city in a buggy and of course discovered what every parent of young children finds out – that pavement kerbs do not lend themselves to wheeling buggies across busy roads, that childcare facilities are few and far between and that travelling on public transport with very young children and associated equipment can be a nightmare. All of this stared me in the face because my needs determined my perception of what was present or, in this case, absent in my environment.

To take a workplace example, if a manager is made redundant and desperately wants to find a new job, he may notice, in a way he never did before, all his neighbours setting off each morning in their cars to go to their place of work while he remains at home. If he is successful and returns to work with another employer he will probably stop noticing everyone leaving their houses at about the same time as him – a different set of needs will now be organising his field of perception, such as remembering to pack some important papers for a meeting.

How then might this notion be useful to you as a coach? The most relevant is that a client's dominant needs will inevitably influence issue selection in coaching sessions. Clients bring what matters most to them at the time. If clients have a promotion board coming up soon they may be acutely conscious of previous interview experiences, particularly if they haven't gone well. They will probably want to go back over these experiences and use the coaching space to prepare and feel as confident as possible about the selection process.

The final proposition on the list refers to learning through the examination of here-and-now experience. This is what is meant by working in the present – a hallmark of the Gestalt approach. If you take a moment to think about any typical organisational setting it will soon become evident how rarely this happens.

If you were to observe most boardroom or senior management team discussions you would hear discussions about the past and the future but little attention to what is happening now in the room. Even when groups have undertaken lengthy team development processes, which produce an intellectual understanding of the difference between task/content and process, content invariably wins out. People focus on the *out there* agenda even if there is little energy for it or when individuals have switched off. Imagine, then, if someone in that group asks the simple question: 'what do we think is happening here right now?' In all likelihood the whole atmosphere of the meeting would change. Initially there might be more discomfort and tension, but the engagement level would probably rise considerably.

Similarly, in a coaching session, if clients are recounting a story of an imminent restructure that will affect their own position in the organisation you might ask the classic Gestalt question: 'and what are you aware of right now as you tell me this?' This would probably deepen clients' connections to what they are really thinking and feeling about it. They might be surprised at how much stronger their feelings are about this event and recognise the greater significance this has for them.

Another focus of here-and-now learning is the coach-client relationship. By focusing on what is happening in the moment your clients may learn something about how they characteristically behave elsewhere. Using the immediate moment provides a constant flow of feedback opportunities that have directness about them. If, for example, clients are endeavouring to change an aspect of their interpersonal connection such as listening better to others, it will be both helpful and supportive if you give them immediate feedback when you notice it happening, or not happening, in the coaching session itself.

How change takes place and the meaning of resistance

By now it will be evident that your job as a coach is not to take someone somewhere. Indeed if you try to do that you will most likely engender greater resistance than already exists. This is known as the paradox of change, articulated by Beisser (1970), and it is fundamental to the Gestalt approach.

This states that one must first fully experience *what is*, one's current reality, before attempting to change things. Beisser argued that the more one tries to be who one is not, the more one stays the same. A key Gestalt premise is that full awareness of current reality spontaneously leads to change. Perls (1969), a cofounder of Gestalt therapy, believed that awareness itself is curative.

This powerful notion first found its way into coaching through the work of Gallwey (2000) who put it this way:

> The first step in this better way to change lies in a non-judgemental acknowledgement of things as they are. Paradoxically, it is conscious acceptance of oneself and one's actions as they are that frees up both incentive and the capacity for spontaneous change.

Working from this premise about how change takes place has radical, far-reaching implications and for many people turns their view of change upside down. Many people, consciously or not, seek to bypass or cut through others' arguments and defences in order to assert their own view of reality. They are then dismayed, irritated and frustrated when people don't do what they expected them to do.

If we believe that change is difficult then it follows that people will feel ambivalent about it. They may see the benefits but are often acutely aware of the costs and losses. They may also have little confidence that they will be able to change.

In Kegan and Lahey's *How the Way we Talk can Change the Way we Work* (2001), there is an apt reference to the issue of resistance to change.

> The late William Perry, a favourite teacher and precious colleague of ours at Harvard, was a gifted trainer of therapists, counsellors and consultants. 'Whenever someone comes to me for help', he used to say, 'I listen very hard and ask myself, what does this person really want – and what will they do to keep from getting it?' As Bill's wry words suggest, if we want deeper understanding of the prospect of change, we must pay closer attention to our own powerful inclinations not to change.

From this perspective resistance is meaningful and in a practical way this makes our work easier. There is little point in pushing the river. Instead we need to recognise and validate resistance as a form of creative expression and adjustment. Without it people would be open to being manipulated and exploited.

If we really believe in respect for people then we must let them make up their own minds and find their own ways. This is, after all, not just at the heart of Gestalt philosophy; it is also a fundamental principle of coaching. The job of the coach is to help clients to discover who they are, what they want and need, and how they can find more productive, healthy ways to meet those needs.

Zinker (1994) summarises the paradoxes of change succinctly and elegantly:

1. If you support what is, and not what should be, change will take place.
2. If you support resistance to change, little resistance will be encountered and change will take place.

Awareness and change

The starting point for change is to fully appreciate *what is* – current reality – and that is achieved by raising awareness. So what do we mean by awareness? Nevis (1987) defines it in this way:

> By awareness I mean the knowing or cognisance that derives from observation of self and other. The process of becoming aware is simply that of using all of our senses in an alert, attentive way. Through our senses – seeing, hearing, feeling, smelling – we become conscious of what is happening to us and around us.

Expressed in this way it seems fairly obvious, simple and straightforward. We use the full range of our human senses to notice and connect with what is happening in ourselves and others. Yet for much of the time our general awareness level is somewhat poor. We miss so much of what is going on within us and around us. We don't always recognise the impact of events on ourselves or the impact we have on others.

Nevis's definition tells us that our innate human equipment – our senses – is the route to awareness-raising but this doesn't fully capture what awareness is. Polster and Polster's (1973) definition adds some further elements:

> Awareness is an ongoing process, readily available at all times, rather than a sporadic illumination that can be achieved – like an insight – only at special moments or under special conditions. It is always there ... ready to be tapped into when needed ... furthermore, focusing on one's awareness keeps one absorbed in the present situation.

This is an encouraging statement as it suggests that awareness is not elusive or momentary in the way we might consider insight to be. Rather, it is available to us at any time. This short experiment might reveal more.

Self-awareness

I invite you to consider your own awareness in this moment. Ask yourself: 'what am I aware of in my body?' Do you notice any physical sensations such as hunger, an itch, an ache or a low level of tiredness or discomfort? Are you excited or anxious and, if so, what about? Notice your breathing and whether it is shallow or deep.

Now consider what you see around you in the room in which you are reading this book. Or if you are sitting outside, take in the environment around you. What do you see? Does anything stand out for you? Don't analyse it, just notice it. Also, what can you hear – a clock ticking, a door being closed in the next room, the hum of a computer? If you're outside, notice the sounds of the birds, the traffic passing by or a dog barking. Take in the smells, the vapours and aromas in your environment. We don't often take the time for all this. Now take stock of your thoughts. What are you thinking right now? When you are ready, look into yourself and discover what you are feeling right now. Are you happy, content, enjoying the moment? Are you bored, frustrated, confused, or disappointed?

These are just a selection of what you can be aware of. When you are in the normal run of things take a moment to observe your inner dialogue, the voice inside you that is planning, organising, making lists, dreaming, fantasising, worrying, or trying to remember something.

Social awareness

Up to this point I have asked you to focus on your internal awareness. So how does this work at the interpersonal and social level? Here is just a top-level review of what you can be aware of in your workplace interactions. Firstly, you can become more attuned to communication patterns and styles. Take for example a meeting – how much engagement, energy and interest appears to be in the room? What are people doing? Are they looking at each other, listening, or typing notes about something completely different onto their laptop? Who talks, who doesn't? Who has impact and who hasn't? Is the atmosphere dull and lethargic or fun and energised? Do some individuals speak for a long time? Do others deflect, switch off, and get irritated? Is there a joker in the group or someone who plays the role of keeping things light and cheerful?

Is difference acknowledged or denied, is conflict encouraged or suppressed? How does leadership operate? What is the level of EI being displayed in the room? How are different people playing the power dynamics? These are just some of the many things that we can become attuned to at the interpersonal level.

The focus on the here-and-now

If we are interested in helping people become more aware of themselves and others, then this requires a focus on the here and now. Discovering what we want and need happens in the 'now'. Getting stuck or confused happens in the 'now'. Making new choices, taking significant decisions and creating new solutions all happen in the 'now'. Observing the relational interactions in a meeting occurs in the 'now'.

This is not to deny the importance of past events. From a Gestalt perspective however, it is not so much the past event *per se* that is important; rather what effect it is having in the present situation. If, for example, I have had a number of negative experiences with previous bosses and I have been unable to gain closure around them, I may now treat my current boss with distrust. By increasing my awareness in the present moment I may discover and learn more about how my current behaviour has echoes in my past. My behaviour becomes more meaningful to me and I recognise that actually my new boss is a completely different individual, the circumstances are now very different, and I don't need or want to replay an old pattern. Awareness in the 'now' produces the possibility of behaviour change going forwards.

So how can you help your clients become more here-and-now focused? This is most likely to be achieved by asking questions that raise awareness. Examples of these are: 'What are you aware of right now?' 'What are you thinking?' 'What are you feeling?' 'What do you notice in yourself?' 'What do you want?' 'How might you get that?' 'What's happening for you right now?'

All these questions have the same common factors. The first is that they are *how* and *what* questions. *Why* questions tend to take people into explaining and justifying themselves, which may not lead to heightened awareness. The second is that they are present tense. They are located in the 'now' and are likely to produce more direct contact with immediate thoughts, feelings and needs.

It's important to recognise that most people are rarely asked these types of questions and therefore may experience some initial surprise. They may feel that you have put them on the spot – asked for an answer that they don't seem to possess. They may experience a mixture of apprehension and excitement at being pushed that little bit further than they are used to.

Helping your clients to use their full range of senses in the here and now is an important aspect of the coaching process. Part of your role is to act as an educator and a guide in awareness raising. If you are looking for a methodology then the capacity to work in the here and now is an essential dimension to it. For many coaches-in-training and indeed more experienced practitioners, this is a critical area of skill development.

Bringing yourself into the coaching relationship

Being fully present is the starting point for building good connection and this requires you to be authentic – be who you are and use your presence creatively. To be authentic may mean bringing more of yourself to your work. A question every coach might usefully ask is 'how much do you bring of yourself to your work?' And just as importantly, 'which parts of yourself don't you bring?' The answers to these questions can suggest important directions for your personal development. For some coaches it can be the more provocative aspects such as challenge and assertiveness. For others it can be the powerful relationship building elements like empathy and warmth. Being able to connect with more aspects of yourself and to bring them authentically into the coaching relationship can make a profound difference to the quality and depth of your work.

The use of presence

Coaching presence is not a neutral presence. You are there to affect things and have impact. Nevis (1987) describes presence as the 'living embodiment of knowledge: the theories and practices believed to be essential to bring about change in people are manifested, symbolized, or implied in the presence of the consultant.' What he is referring to is the notion of coach as a learning model and this implies standing for something.

From a Gestalt perspective there are a number of values and assumptions that most practitioners share. They are listed extensively by Zinker (1994) and include: high functioning, efficient problem solving, self-regulation, self-validation, flexible boundaries, authenticity, greater connection, goal achievement, growth and balance. It would be hard to imagine a more appropriate set of values for psychologically focused coaches.

I am not equating presence with style or charisma: this is not about being a shining star around which everyone gathers to bask in your reflected rays. Presence is denoted in a multitude of ways from the loud, gregarious, outgoing, and cheerful to the quiet, thoughtful and considered. It is less about how you look or what you dress and sound like, although these do play a part. It's far more about the extent to which how you are and who you are is in accord with what you are trying to be and do. In other words it's about the degree of integration between what you say you are about and how you act in the world. Where that integration is strong, a powerful and compelling impact is usually the result. Conversely, when there is a significant gap between words and actions, presence is diminished.

The critical challenge for any coach is to live what you stand for, not just talk about it. The role modelling aspect of your work may be every bit as important as your most elegant intervention. When you model behaviours to do with self-awareness, awareness of others, non-judgemental interest, and real contact it will evoke a positive reaction in your clients. They will get interested, curious and engaged. They may have been unconsciously looking for a supportive lead to give themselves greater permission to be who they really are.

The nature of support

An important aspect of your role as a coach is to provide enough external support to supplement your client's internal self-support. But what do we really mean by support? Many books of this kind typically emphasise the importance of deep, respectful, compassionate, non-judgemental listening as the critical success factor.

Certainly, if you've been on the receiving end of this quality of listening you will appreciate just how important it is. What gives it that special quality is the nature and depth of support emanating from it. For example, I may tell you about a troubling issue affecting me in my work context to which I have given much thought. My dilemma is that I still don't seem to be able to resolve it and I feel frustrated and somewhat hopeless about it. There are many ways that you might respond, some of which will be helpful, some not. In my own particular case I am unlikely to find uninvited advice helpful; in fact it will probably leave me irritated and thinking that you haven't bothered to listen deeply enough. You might try to get me to see that my thinking or behaviour is faulty and, of course, it may be. However, if you do this too quickly and without first acknowledging and validating how I see the world then I may become defensive. On the other hand, if you stretch yourself that bit further and really try to get into my shoes, and see the world through my eyes rather than your own, then I am likely to feel heard and understood. I'll feel that you have 'got it'. This will enable me to relax with you and put down my guard. I won't be waiting for you to try to change me or impose your views and opinions onto mine. I will have no need to resist you.

This is at the heart of how Gestalt practitioners believe change takes place, and why so often it doesn't. It is as much about the process of change as it is about the practitioner as the agent of change. And the most important part of that process is to really understand and validate your client's experiential world. If clients feel that this is happening, their attention and energy can move from being on guard to being more open to new possibilities – to growth and change.

Listening and validating how people see their world is not, however, the same as agreeing with everything they say. In coaching there is often a time and place for challenge. However, if this is done from a working alliance built on respect and acknowledgement, your clients will experience less threat and therefore less need to protect themselves.

How you view challenge is an important issue in itself. Some coaches see challenge as an opposite of support rather than a dimension of it. Support includes challenge just as it incorporates deep listening, respect and empathic connection. There will be times when the most supportive thing you can do for your clients is to challenge them. Many executives both expect it and seek it. They may not experience being supported unless they have been challenged.

Some clients find it difficult to let in support. They may have a long-standing pattern of self-sufficiency reinforced by years of life in the executive fast lane where senior people are expected to look to themselves for motivation and self-maintenance. When they are then offered the support of executive coaching, they don't know how best to use it. They are not familiar with having an external resource and may be embarrassed about revealing doubts, uncertainties and the vulnerability inherent in the client role. They are far more used to sitting in your seat asking probing questions of their managers.

Self-support

Whilst some clients may need to learn more about how to derive more support from their external environment – their coach, colleagues, boss, family and friends – they may also need to grow their internal capacity for self-support. Now it's important to state that self-support is not another way of describing *being an island*. Many executives already feel that they have to do that because there is usually insufficient support in their external environment. Self-support is not about being a rock with no needs of one's own.

Instead, it is about using awareness to notice one's emerging needs and learning how to meet those needs in healthy, productive ways. For the executive client this might mean taking some extra time out from a busy schedule to find a quiet, reflective, nurturing space. It may mean withdrawal from contact with demanding colleagues or customers in order to focus more on oneself. It may be as simple as getting more rest, eating better or losing oneself in a novel. For others it may be more energetic than that and involve travel, adventure or achieving a physical challenge.

An important implication of this work is that when clients become more attuned to their needs they can become less tolerant of some of the circumstances of their lives. Whereas previously they may have felt a low level of dissatisfaction yet put up with it, they may become less inclined to do so. Instead they may find themselves questioning whether their work situation is really fulfilling their needs.

When people are supported well enough to examine their work and wider lives you can't be sure where it will take them. It is a well known fact that one of the outcomes of executive coaching is that a percentage of clients choose to leave their jobs; a smaller number elect to leave corporate life altogether. This doesn't necessarily mean an inescapable conflict although it may do on some occasions. It can lead to a healthy and positive rewriting of the boundaries, which can be good news for both parties.

13 Achieving closure around issues

Self regulation

Perls (1969) believed that people have a natural tendency to create a sense of balance or *homeostasis* which calls on our capacity to effectively self-regulate. Balance is maintained by attending to internal needs as they emerge and to external demands from the environment. Perls' view was that we are in a constant process of meeting, or failing to gratify these needs and demands, and he referred to this as *organismic self-regulation*. When we meet our needs we experience a sense of equilibrium: when we don't there is incompleteness and a sense of something being unfinished.

The cyclical nature of how we self-regulate is at the core of Gestalt theory and is known as the Cycle of Experience. So how do we identify those needs in the first place? In Gestalt theory this is known as the *figure-ground* process.

Figure and ground

A *figure* is whatever occupies the foreground of your interest right now. It might be this book, an emerging need for food, the sun on your face, a headache or the worry that just won't seem to go away. A *figure* can be what you are looking at, listening to or thinking about. It can be the task you are engaged with or the problem you are currently grappling with. It's whatever is taking your attention now.

Ground, on the other hand, is all those things that go to comprise our background. As you read this book your *figure* may be the interest, intrigue or frustration you are experiencing with these ideas. Your *ground* may include the fact that you will shortly need to drive to the station to pick up your partner, walk to the school to meet your children, or go out to an important work meeting. At some point, that will replace this book as your *figure* and the book will become *ground*.

In a deeper sense your *ground* also includes your bedrock, your ways of seeing and acting in the world, your habitual patterns, the way you construct your reality, some of which you may be conscious of, some not. This bedrock provides the lens or filters for how you approach or view new *figures*. If for example your *ground* includes a belief that you cannot understand complex theories then you might quickly give up on the assimilation of new concepts.

Similarly, if you have always believed that you are poor at sport then you may avoid opportunities in the present to try a new activity. And, if you have not achieved closure around criticism you received on a regular basis when young you may now, as an adult, struggle to hear feedback because you interpret anything negative as intolerable criticism.

Learning, and therefore change, from a Gestalt perspective has to do with changing the *ground*, not just the *figure*. Otherwise you will need to go over the same figural changes repeatedly. From this perspective, *learning as a change in our ground*, it becomes clearer why developmental work requires greater depth than you might first think.

From a coaching perspective, this has a particular significance. If coaching simply deals with today's issues and problems (*figures*), then it is in danger of being little more than an effective problem-solving tool. When coaching works at two levels – helping clients solve current problems while also developing them as individuals – it reveals a far greater potentiality.

As a coach you will always be confronted by your client's figural issues – what matters most to them right now. When you look back, however, on a period of coaching with a client I imagine that you would want to feel that the client has also grown as a leader and as a person. This requires a change in clients' *ground*; the substance of who they are.

The Cycle of Experience

A fundamental Gestalt premise is that people can more readily organise themselves into new ways of seeing and acting through heightened awareness. Out of this stronger awareness we energise ourselves and take actions that lead to the achievement of important goals. In completing these cycles we assimilate learning and get closure around issues. Conversely, our actions may not lead to our desired results if they are not based on full awareness. Instead they may look promising at the outset but then prove to be insubstantial, superficial or downright erroneous later on.

The Cycle of Experience is a central orienting model of Gestalt practitioners. Needs (*figures*) arise and are satisfied producing a withdrawal of interest in a cyclical or wave-like rhythmic pattern. It is typically represented as a seven-stage process beginning with sensation, moving through awareness and energy mobilisation to action and contact producing resolution/ closure and withdrawal of interest.

If you relate this to figure-ground process, the notion is that new *figures* form or emerge from the background and if you attend to them in this natural sequence then you will achieve closure around them and they will become part of your *ground*.

The cycle represents a model of healthy functioning where needs arise

Figure 13.1. The Cycle of Experience.

and are in turn satisfied. For the most part people complete cycles of experience in an easy, uncomplicated way especially when it comes to meeting their physical needs. I qualify this with the words *for the most part* because, even at the physical level, we do not always engage in a healthy flow. Sometimes, for very good reasons, we go without sufficient food, sleep, exercise or relaxation. Our self-regulation is not what it might be. The complexities and demands of modern lives mean that we skip meals, burn the candle at both ends or just feel too tired to bother with exercise.

At the social and emotional levels the process is inevitably more complex. Meeting our needs for connection and intimacy poses real challenges for many people. A very common social/emotional *figure* in the workplace is to feel included by the boss and fellow team members. We like to be informed about what is happening and feel that we have been consulted. When this doesn't happen we can become distressed and distracted.

In Gestalt terms this is what is known as *incomplete Gestalts*, more popularly termed unfinished business. Unfinished business is being stuck somewhere on the Cycle yet unable to fully withdraw attention from it. The issue just keeps gnawing away. Perhaps it may seem to go away for a while, only later to be restimulated by an event or person in present time.

In an earlier section I referred to unfinished business as one of the most common issues brought to executive coaching. Here I explore what is really meant by it and how you, as a coach, might work with it.

Unfinished business

The notion of getting *closure around issues* is a key objective in Gestalt. Gestalt theory suggests that human beings have a need to complete experiences and to achieve closure. If something shocks, upsets or surprises us we go around and around the situation internally or in conversation with others to try to make sense and meaning from it. If we can, then it fades into the background; if we can't, it remains active.

Given that that there will always be new needs (*figures*) competing for our attention it is inevitable that we won't be able to achieve closure in an easy, sequential manner. In any event, some *figures* are just too complex and emotionally loaded for us to reach closure in a simple, comfortable or speedy way. They contain high levels of significance such as when we feel let down by a colleague or we fail to land a job that we believed was ours by right.

In the work context, unfinished business is a critical factor in both individual and team performance. Competent, high-achieving people leave jobs each day due to unresolved issues with their organisation, typically around their boss. Some teams are sinking under the weight of their unfinished business. One of the key characteristics of dysfunctional teams is the amount, complexity and depth of unfinished business running within team relationships.

It would be clearer if all this was an outcome of the present set of circumstances and people in the scenario. Unfortunately, it's rarely as straightforward as that. People in the present context may be acting out and replaying conflicts that belong to the past but which have triggers in the present.

Working with unfinished business

Because there is so rarely enough support in the environment to open up and face our unfinished business we may not even believe it's possible. Instead we may consider it something we'll just have to learn to live with. Its importance may not register on us anyway and we may not be aware of it leaking out through barbed comments or thinly disguised sarcasm in our everyday interactions.

For some people a time may come when it screams so strongly for attention that they finally go looking for help. This can be the moment in someone's life when they choose to enter coaching or therapy. The noise has just got so loud that it can't be ignored any more.

The prospect of addressing unfinished business is generally daunting to most people, which only underlines just how important it is to provide an adequate level of support for those daring to open up their issues. People are often taken aback by their previously suppressed feelings and worry that if they do lift the lid further then the floodgates will open. Although this rarely happens, it is a common fear in the client and indeed in the less experienced coach.

Retroflection

Gestalt has some useful concepts that describe how and why people struggle to get closure around issues and thus accumulate unfinished business. The first of these is retroflection. This literally means to turn inward upon oneself. Typically, we retroflect when we believe it would be unwise, even dangerous, to speak or act out what we inwardly wish to say or do. In the workplace, people retroflect for many different reasons including career or political considerations and there may be a great deal of wisdom in this, particularly where a boss is known for holding grudges.

We learn to retroflect from an early stage of life. Children learn within their families what thoughts, feelings and actions are acceptable and validated and which are not. Breaking the rules can result in physical and/or psychological punishment and young people learn to hold their tongues. In families where feelings of any kind have been suppressed and acceptable personal expression is limited to sensible, rational, intellectual conversation it can be difficult in later life for offspring of that family to express their emotions.

There is no doubt that a certain amount of bottling up of unexpressed views and feelings is simply part of being human and has some virtue in it. We may not wish to hurt the other person, it may be a bad time, or the individual may simply be unavailable to deal with directly. However, the consequences of turning inwards can be twofold. We can get into a spiral of self-berating behaviour, which can lead to depression. Secondly, it can get in the way of full, meaningful contact. Instead of being easy and comfortable in the other person's company we either minimise contact, because it's too painful or, if we have to be in regular communication, we go through the motions but real contact is limited.

Introjection

Introjection is a Gestalt term that refers to the process of swallowing whole the beliefs, attitudes, values and edicts of other significant others. This happens especially in early life and many of these introjections are useful, even necessary. When the parent tells their youngster not to put his or her finger into an electrical wall socket this is an introjection that one would want to stick. Similarly, at the social and community level, there are countless norms that societies need their citizens to introject in order to hold together and function well. Driving on the correct side of the road would be a simple example.

In adult life organisations seek to instil certain values and *modi operandi* on their staff, which they want to be introjected without too much debate and argument. Customer service is an example of this. Working to the leadership agenda and accepting management decisions are others.

The negative consequences of introjection occur when internalised shoulds and should-nots, oughts and ought-nots prevent people from being able to seek and achieve satisfaction to important personal needs. The young girl who grows up being told it is selfish to put one's own needs forward and instead that she should look after others may encounter difficulties later in life allowing herself to get her own intimacy needs met.

One of the important implications of the notion of introjection is that we may never fully know how much, or little, of what we think and believe about the world is simply undigested material handed down from parents, teachers and other authority figures from our past. Have we really examined our belief and attitudinal systems or are we simply regurgitating someone else's world view with all its merits and flaws?

From this perspective we can see that self-development is really about discovering what we believe and who we really want to be. In the process we will inevitably hold on to much of what we have introjected but will know that we have made it our own. We may also abandon some of what we have come to believe – a process that may be both liberating and painful.

Introjection is a particularly helpful notion when addressing unfinished business but also when you are coaching clients on meaning-making issues.

In both cases the starting point is to help your clients arrive at a deeper understanding of their shoulds and oughts. This will raise awareness of how their internal scripts, perhaps until now relatively unexamined, may be holding them back from fulfilling their potential. Classic examples of introjects which can have a self-limiting result are: 'don't get above your station in life', 'know your place', and 'you should just be happy with your lot'.

How introjects are formed is an interesting subject but to the coach the most pertinent issue is not why they are there or where they have come from – it's what impact they now have on your clients' capacity to form meaningful relationships, find out what they want from work and life and go about fulfilling themselves as people.

If one of your client's introjects is that *one shouldn't challenge your seniors*, and this a very common introject, then the client may keep feelings of being upset arising out of a slight quarrel with the boss unspoken in order to avoid conflict. Instead of tackling it, the client may retroflect.

This is where introjects and retroflects connect. *I should not challenge my seniors'* leads to *I had better keep my upset feelings inside because it is not acceptable to say something.* To complicate things further, if your clients have introjected that having angry feelings is 'bad' then they may castigate themselves for having those feelings in the first place.

Coaching options

From a tactical perspective there are two intervention points. The first is to focus on the retroflecting. As the coach you can use awareness-raising questions that bring your clients to the recognition that they are holding back on something that is important to them. You might help them see how this is leaving them feeling stuck, dissatisfied and lacking closure around the issue. This will inevitably highlight the choices that they are making and not making. As ever, the vital coaching caveat is that it is for the clients to decide what, if anything, they will do about this. However, as the coach, you are likely to want to point out the costs of retroflecting. The working relationship may be less honest, committed and open. Your client may be feeling miserable and unhappy.

Undoing the retroflection involves speaking out what has been turned inwards and this will probably put your clients more in touch with what they are really feeling about it. In Gestalt there is a classic technique for helping someone to do this within the relative safety of the coaching session. It is known as the *chairwork* exercise. Clients are invited to bring the protagonist to whom things have not been fully expressed and to imagine that individual sitting in the empty chair right now. Clients then discover what they have to say to that person and, in the process, typically find out just how strongly they have been feeling about the unfinished business. It is often a great release for the clients as they finally get things off of their chest that they may have been carrying for weeks, months or even years.

This raises the question of whether your client will then need to go back and do the same with the real person. On some occasions the cathartic benefit of speaking it out in the session can be enough. The client may experience a sufficient sense of closure from this process alone. On others occasions your client may need to have a conversation with the actual person, face to face. Having expressed feelings through the chairwork exercise the client is likely to feel more in control and therefore more confident going into this situation.

There are two health warnings that go with this exercise. The first is that the chairwork technique may seem very strange to some executive clients and should only be used after careful consideration. Another way to achieve a similar result but with less theatre is to ask your client to: 'imagine your colleague is here in the room right now, what would you like to say to him?' This can be a good enough opener for your client to speak out what has been bottling up. As clients do this it can also be helpful to ask them to say what they are feeling as they say these things.

The second cautionary note is that this powerful process should not be used without first experiencing it several times yourself as the client and then learning how to use it in a properly supervised training situation with tutors or facilitators who genuinely understand the technique and who can can provide proper guidance.

The other focus of intervention, and this may have more benefits in the longer term, is to help your clients more fully appreciate their introjections. The reason for this is that although the client will derive benefit from expressing feelings around a previously held-in issue, if she doesn't understand the deeper dynamic then she may continue to retroflect in future situations that contain similar features.

The process of exploring introjects requires care and sensitivity. To you, as the coach, the introject may sound like faulty thinking such as when clients say that they shouldn't challenge people in authority because it's wrong to do so. You may strongly disagree with their thinking and firmly challenge it. In turn your clients may find it hard to justify the logic of their viewpoint but nevertheless feel strongly attached to it. The act of challenging the thinking implicit in the introject will not always result in your client reevaluating it or letting it go.

There are several reasons for this. The first is that introjections are typically long standing and deep rooted. They don't disappear as a result of one moment of insight. This would suggest a far more rational explanation of how people operate than is really the case. The second, and this is perhaps more fundamental, is that our critical introjects are tied into our key relationships with the most important people and influencers in our lives. Our attachment to our introjects is about our attachment to those people. Most often this operates at an unconscious level. Your clients will rarely be able to articulate this unless they have undertaken a lengthy period of self-examination through a process such as psychotherapy.

The relevance of this to you as the coach is that if you strongly challenge what is, to your clients a fundamental belief system, then they may experience you as fundamentally challenging not just them, but also their mother, father, spiritual guide or important friend or mentor. In suggesting that the clients may be wrong, you are implicitly implying that those who influenced them were wrong also. Seen from this perspective it is hardly surprising that this is almost certain to produce resistance.

This is why it is so important to tread carefully when working with introjects. You will probably recognise very quickly if you step too heavily into this territory. Your client may react strongly or withdraw from you and switch off. You might sense that you have overstepped the mark and notice some apprehension in yourself. When this happens the important thing is to sensitively acknowledge it, apologise and back off. If your clients are ready to go there they will tell you. The critical issue is that the power is with the client.

Much of what is implied here is to do with your stance as a coach rather than technique. The critical element of that stance is respect. If your clients experience this from you then they will take more risks even if some of these lead to difficult moments. They will also be more likely to forgive you for the occasional misplaced steps.

Working from a respectful position will often provide sufficient support for your clients to think more deeply about the impact that their introjects are having in their work and wider life. This can be part of that deeper process of discovering who they are, what they want and whether they will go about getting it. It will be so much easier if they don't feel that they are going against their precious people to achieve it.

14 The coach's guidance systems

The Cycle of Experience as an orienting model

The awareness stage

Imagine a one-one coaching session. You are 5 minutes, maybe 10 minutes, into the session with a client. Already several themes have been raised and you are sitting there wondering which, if any of these, is the important one to focus on. How do you know? How can you know? It's perfectly possible that you haven't yet arrived at the issue or theme that will take precedence in the session.

In this situation the challenge for you as the coach is to be patient and trust the process. This is a time when you need to just tolerate your own confusion and live with a degree of ambiguity. Staying grounded, dealing with your own anxiety and avoiding a premature rush to fix things can be one of the most difficult aspects of the coaching role.

The coach's job at this stage is to stay focused on the *awareness* point of the Cycle. Questions that raise awareness are the coach's staple tool and now's the time to use them creatively and purposefully. Some coaches also use awareness heightening exercises at this stage such as brainstorming, mind mapping or experiments created in the moment.

If you stay focused at the awareness stage of the Cycle then *figures* will almost certainly form. Some may lack shape, form, interest and vitality. These will tend to come and go without leaving a strong impression until something more clearly emerges from the *ground*. How will you know when this happens? Firstly you may notice a qualitatively different engagement with the issue on the part of your client and secondly, you will probably notice a different reaction in yourself. You may hear yourself saying 'aha' inside your head.

You may be wondering what meaning to ascribe to those earlier *figures*. Were the clients aware that they were not their most pressing issues? Or was it more a question of needing to thrash around for awhile before finding a more meaningful issue? It could be either. Sometimes clients know what they most need to address but are not yet ready to go there. On many more occasions people simply need time to get in touch with their needs. They may also need to reconnect with you first and establish stronger contact before going to a deeper place.

In Nevis's (1987) book on organisational consulting he suggests a number of different intervention strategies, each geared to different stages of the cycle. At the awareness stage he advocates that you – 'attend, observe and selectively share observations of what you see, hear and feel'. This is to act as 'self as mirror'. You feed back what you think will be the most pertinent observations to raise the awareness of your client. This can be at the level of non-verbal communication, or can be focused around behaviours. Tone of voice, bodily gestures, eye contact and communication style are all examples of this kind of feedback. In the coaching session you may be struck by an apparent discrepancy between what your clients are saying and how they are saying it. They may be talking about being excited about an event and yet sound flat and lacking in energy. Alternatively they may say that they need to do something or change something yet leave you feeling unconvinced.

Nevis also includes the coach's use of self as an awareness raising intervention when he suggests that you – 'attend to your own experience (feelings, sensations, thoughts) and selectively share these.' This is to draw on what is being evoked in you through connection with your client. You might find yourself feeling moved, inspired, saddened, confused or anxious. You may be immediately interested and may want to discover more; or you may find that your curiosity and energy is barely aroused at all. All of this is information which you might draw on as a source of intervention.

The energy mobilisation and action stages

Clients may turn up to their coaching sessions, be physically present, and yet you get the sense that they don't really want to work or engage. This type of session lacks energy and doesn't seem to get off the ground. This can be confusing and anxiety provoking for the coach who knows that in order to dance both parties need to take some steps, or at least get onto the dance floor. In your anxiety you may try to do all the steps to make up for the lack of energy from your client. Sometimes this can spark things off but in the longer run it may be counterproductive as it can set a pattern of interaction that relies on you providing the energy rather than your client.

Nevis's intervention strategy at this stage is 'to focus on energy in the client system and the emergence or lack of themes or issues; to support mobilisation of client energy (joining) so that something happens.'

Working from a Gestalt approach implies working with the emerging process. This often requires patience to allow time for themes to become strong enough figures around which energy and interest mobilises. When a clear theme does emerge it can be a great relief for the coach and the client. There is a purposeful, meaningful focus. The job of the coach from this point is to support that mobilised energy so that the client moves to the action stage of the Cycle.

Action can mean a whole host of things. It may be simply talking more about an issue and going further into it. It may be an experiment such as role-playing a conversation that the client intends to have with a colleague. The Gestalt chairwork exercise might be used at this stage.

The contact stage

It will usually be obvious when clients' energy around an issue has mobilised sufficiently to propel them into taking action. Where there was previously a sense of stuckness there is now a greater sense of engagement. Productive work will usually be evident and it's likely that you, as the coach, will also feel more interested, involved and enlivened.

It is now critical to get to the core of the issue and for clients to connect with it in sufficient depth to be in full and meaningful contact with its significance to them. If your clients skirt around the edges then they may derive little value from the session. This is the time when sessions invariably need to go deeper.

There are several ways in which you, as the coach, can assist in this process. It might be the time for stronger challenge, warmer support or recognition and appreciation. It might be that you need to probe that little more or facilitate the expression of feelings.

Nevis refers to the coaching intervention strategy at the contact stage in the following way – *to facilitate clear, meaningful, heightened contact (including their contact with you).*

What he means by *contact with you* is that clients may have a need to say something to you perhaps in recognition of the value they place on your support, care or skill. Alternatively, they may choose to tell you about something they have been unhappy about in the coaching relationship.

The withdrawal and closure stage

This is a time when clients may want to reflect on what has been learnt and any actions that may need to follow. Your role as the coach is to help them draw meaning from the session. It can be useful for some clients if you summarise what you understand to have been the pertinent aspects of the process and, in so doing, bring the session together.

It's important not to overwhelm clients at this point by trying to capture everything. If your clients have been to a deeper place then they may prefer a quieter, more reflective space. If the coach gets too busy then much of it will go straight over their head. Your challenge as a coach is to tune into what is needed and remember that less can be more.

If the coaching theme has been around a strategic business issue and you have compiled an action plan including next steps, then clients may wish to have this reiterated in order to organise their thoughts before leaving the session.

Nevis refers to the tasks at this stage in this way – *to help the client achieve heightened awareness of their overall process in completing units of work and to achieve closure around problem areas of unfinished business.*

When clients become more conscious of their own process they can more effectively monitor whether they are gaining closure around issues, a critical factor in self-regulation. It doesn't necessarily follow that they will complete units of work but it is certainly more likely that they will become aware when they don't. They may then self-correct by bringing themselves back and using their growing capacity to self-coach.

This is the use of the Cycle of Experience as the orienting framework. It acts like a compass to give a bearing on where you are. Honouring this natural process, however, is not just for your client; it's also for you as the coach so that you properly look after yourself. When you are stuck or confused go back to awareness raising. Trust that fuller awareness will invariably provide the key that unlocks the door. Learn how to tolerate the inevitable confusion implicit in this work and avoid prematurely rushing for solutions and action. Discover more about what it really feels like to be in strong contact and how to facilitate it. Remember how important it is to take the learning from the withdrawal stage before attending to the next thing. Take time for reflection and satisfaction. This is how you too will grow both as practitioner and as a person.

The use of self as instrument of change

Imagine the following coaching scenario. You have arrived feeling open to meeting and working with Mike, a new client, and you're curious to see what emerges in your early interaction with him. Of course you want to understand his story- and his issues, and pay full attention to the content of the session. But there is so much more to pick up than these elements. To use yourself as instrument means to tune into your personal reactions to being with Mike. These will probably be evoked by Mike's style of relating. The impact this has on you is essential information. Does he take over and try to manage you or does he keep himself distant and watch each move and response before venturing forward again? Does he talk and talk, leaving little room for you to come in? Does he appear to ignore your attempts to get in? What are your thoughts and feelings in response to him? Do you find yourself warming to him, interested and engaged? Or do you feel you're only just hanging in there, perhaps bored or frustrated? Do you experience yourself as an 'I' or an

'It' in the interaction? In other words do you feel that he is genuinely trying to meet you or do you feel like an object – that he could be talking to anyone? Do you feel clear about what Mike is saying or overwhelmed by the story and the out surge of information, thoughts and feelings?

At the beginning of the meeting you probably felt grounded, at ease, and comfortable with yourself and with the prospect of meeting Mike. Half an hour into the session are you now experiencing anxiety, and less strong and confident in yourself? Are you asking yourself 'can I work with this man?' or even 'am I really cut out for this work?'

To attend to the story and keep up with the content of a session can be a stretch in the early days for new coaches. Being asked to do that and simultaneously helicopter above yourself to notice your client's style of relating and your own internal thoughts and feelings in reaction, may seem a very challenging proposition. You may be concerned that you will lose some of the detail of the story and miss important pieces of information. This, of course, may happen whether you are a new coach or a more experienced one, although with practice, coaches tend to find that they can increasingly trust themselves to pick up enough of the content.

To use self involves taking the risk of losing some of the words as you change your *figure* from the story to your observations of how your client makes contact, and what is evoked in you. The benefits of taking this risk can be enormous, even transformational in terms of new insights and depth of work.

Firstly, it enables you to collect a rich array of data from what you see out there in the client. You can then open this storehouse and selectively share your observations and in doing so provide rich feedback material to your client. The second relates to your experience of the client. The proposition is this – that your reactions may well reveal something important about how others react to this individual's style of relating and contacting. If your client always describes things in excruciating detail when you meet them then it's not an unrealistic idea that the client may be doing that in work relationships. If the client always seems to calibrate issues at 9 out of 10 and you experience a mixture of panic laced with some incredulity then you are probably not the only one to respond to this person in this way. If you dread the session with a particular client because you are invariably left feeling inadequate afterwards then others may be feeling similarly. If you feel intimidated and in professional danger whilst working with a client then what might that tell you about what others in their work environment are experiencing?

Now we come to perhaps the most difficult part. How do you know if your reactions are simply your personal material – that is, if they say more about your unresolved issues than your client's? Perhaps the client's sharp edge is fine and appropriate to executive life and you just have difficulty with successful, driven, somewhat aggressive people. Perhaps the male executive reminds you of your father, whom you would have never felt able to challenge and question. Instead you found other ways to manage your relationship with him – ways that limited the likelihood of any conflict developing.

The question of whose issue, whose material it is becomes vital when we take on the notion of using self as instrument. It leads inevitably to the importance of personal development and knowing more about self. Coaches who have engaged in little self-examination may well lack sufficient self-awareness to be able to discriminate between their own and their client's issues. The use of self in this case could be harmful or simply way off the mark. This is why it is absolutely essential that those who work more psychologically and incorporate the use of self subject themselves to deeper processes of personal development, preferably in both one-one and group situations.

The purpose of undertaking this deeper self-exploration, in addition to your own personal growth, is that you are better positioned to assess when your inner radar screen reads *own personal material or client's personal material*. The more you understand about your own long-standing, deep-rooted patterns, how you make contact, your assumptions about the world and your own difficult places, the better placed you are to use yourself as an instrument of change; confident that you are acting with an adequate level of self and other awareness. Without that you may always feel shaky and anxious about bringing too much of yourself into the equation.

From a Gestalt perspective the use of self links back into the Cycle of Experience. As a coach do you notice when you switch off or become more alert and interested? Do you notice your energy mobilising around certain themes and issues? Is that because they are your own interests and preferences or can you trust that you are more energised because you are now on a productive theme for your client? Are you conscious of the tension inherent in a situation that has not produced full and meaningful contact? Do you allow yourself to take satisfaction and pleasure from a piece of work that has completed the Cycle? Do you give yourself a space to rest and withdraw before engaging in your next Cycle or do you rush from closure to the next thing?

One critical point remains in this exploration of the use of self – what to do with what's on your internal radar screen? It's one thing to notice it and be confident about making the judgement – who and where is this coming from? It's quite another thing to use this internal data skilfully as the basis for making interventions. Many trainee coaches and those unused to using self initially fear that their intervention will lack finesse or, worse still, confuse the client. Will it sound as if I am talking more about myself? Will it leave the client questioning my competence? Will it weaken my presence if I comment on my feelings of confusion? All of these fears have some grounding and may produce a reluctance in coaches to venture themselves. Using self will usually seem like a risky thing to do. However, this is possibly the highest value intervention you can make and if you take the time and trouble to develop this art then the payoff can be significant. The learning impact can be enormous. It can also deepen the relationship between you and your clients.

So how do you know when and how to articulate your own internal data? Are there rules or guidelines? The first thing to say is that it is not incumbent on you to unload all the contents of your internal storehouse. Instead you may choose to hold back on a great deal of it because it's too poorly formed, the timing is not right, or the relationship is not yet sufficiently robust. Perhaps your client is feeling raw and vulnerable from some tough feedback from a boss or colleagues. Now may not be the best time.

There is also the question of how open clients are to hearing what you might have to say. They may be stuck in *broadcast* mode rather than a *receive* mode. Consideration for where the client is right now becomes an obvious criterion for if and when to use self. Beyond that, you need to be able to clearly articulate your observations in a non-critical, supportive manner and without too much investment in whether they are right. Sometimes the observation will hit the mark and your client will immediately recognise value and learning in what is being offered. On other occasions clients may look a little bewildered – the offering doesn't make a great deal of sense to them. In this case you simply need to leave it and back off gracefully. Good articulation of inner data can take the form of metaphors or images and it is an important feature of Gestalt work to experiment with your own creative ways to express yourself. A useful guideline is to keep the intervention economic on words. If the client is straining to understand it because of its length and complexity then it will probably lack impact.

As with any kind of intervention, whether it is high or low on artistry and elegance, intentionality is always a key factor. If the observation is made with good heart and from considered thought then it is likely to be well received.

In the final analysis it is only through practice that you will improve your capacity to use self. Practice with feedback is better. One of the most obvious places is an advanced practitioner programme that has practice/feedback sessions as a core part of its methodology. Another is to look for opportunities to work in team development or training course situations alongside more experienced coaches who are well versed in using self and can both give you feedback on your interventions as well as articulate their own for your learning purposes.

Summary

The fundamental premises upon which both Gestalt and coaching theory are based have much in common. Both are founded on awareness as the precursor to change and each stresses the paramount importance of choice and personal responsibility.

As Wheeler (in Wheeler and Backman, 1994) rightly suggests:

> to change behaviour, in any lasting and organised way, we have to change our awareness of what the possibilities of satisfaction are in the world, and what the possible and permissible goals and feelings are for ourselves.

Gestalt offers a theory of how change takes place and the meaning of resistance. It presents a framework for understanding healthy functioning and the values and assumptions implicit in good process at both the personal and interpersonal levels.

Beyond that it offers a methodology focused around the here and now, the use of self, and the behavioural skills necessary to intervene effectively at different stages of the Cycle of Experience. This provides the potentiality for facilitating closure around unfinished business and problematic issues. At the level of meaning making it validates people's struggles to get in touch with what they want and need but goes beyond that to help them learn how to use the support available to them in their environment and crucially, to support themselves more effectively .

Finally, in my experience, coaches have quite different reactions to the Gestalt approach. Those who take to it most strongly enjoy the directness of the method where clients are encouraged to *talk to* rather than *talk about*. They are enlivened by the here-and-now focus and the precedence of dialogue over technique. They are also engaged by working with the emerging process much as the modern jazz musician thrives on improvising out of a basic structure. Those who prefer the path to be more clearly laid out may initially struggle until they connect with the common thread that links Gestalt and coaching – that the awareness process is what ultimately creates and facilitates change.

References

Bandura, A. (1997) *Self-Efficacy: The Exercise of Control*. New York: Freeman.

Beisser, A.R. (1970) The paradoxical theory of change, in J. Fagan and I.L. Shepherd (eds) *Gestalt Therapy Now: Theory, Techniques, Applications*. Harmondsworth: Penguin.

Berglas, S. (2002) The very real dangers of executive coaching, *Harvard Business Review*, (June): 87–92.

Casement, P. (1985) *On Learning from the Patient*. Hove: Brunner-Routledge.

Cason, K. and Jaques, E. (1994) *Human Capability*. Falls Church: Cason Hall.

CIPD (2004) *Training and Development 2004*. London: CIPD.

Clarkson, P. (2004) *Gestalt Counselling In Action*. 3rd edn. London: Sage.

Czander, W.M. (1993) *The Psychodynamics of Work and Organizations: Theory and Application*. New York: Guilford Press.

Erikson, E.H. (1959) Identity and the life cycle, *Psychological Issues*, 1: 1–171.

European Mentoring and Coaching Council (2006) *Report of the Standards Research Project*.

Executive Coaching Forum (2004) *The Executive Coaching Handbook*. 3rd edn. Wellesley: Executive Coaching Forum.

Fitzgerald, C. and Garvey Berger, J. (2002) *Executive Coaching: Practices and Perspectives*. Palo Alto: Davies-Black Publishing.

Gallwey, W.T. (1974) *The Inner Game of Tennis*. London: Pan Books.

Gallwey, W.T. (2000) *The Inner Game of Work: Overcoming Mental Obstacles for Maximum Performance*. London: Orion Business Books.

Goldsmith, M., Lyons, L. and Freas A. (2000) *Coaching For Leadership: How the World's Greatest Coaches Help Leaders Learn*. San Francisco: Jossey-Bass/Pfeiffer.

Goleman, D. (1996) *Emotional Intelligence: Why It Can Matter More than IQ*. London: Bloomsbury.

Goleman, D., Boyatzis, R. and Mckee, A. (2002) *The New Leaders: Transforming the Art of Leadership into the Science of Results*. London, Little Brown.

Grant, A.M. (2003) Keeping up with the cheese again! Research as a foundation for professional coaching of the future. Keynote presentation paper: International Coach Federation Conference Symposium. Denver.

Greene, J. and Grant, A.M. (2003) *Solution-focused Coaching: Managing People in a Complex World*. Harlow: Managers.

Hawkins, P. and Shohet, R. (2001) *Supervision in the Helping Professions: An individual, group and organizational approach*. 2nd edn. Maidenhead: Open University Press.

Hubble, M.A., Duncan, B.L. and Miller, S.D. (1999) *The Heart and Soul of Change: What Works in Therapy*. Washington, American Psychological Association.

Kadushin, A. (1976) *Supervision in Social Work*. New York: Columbia University Press.

Kegan, R. (1994) *In Over Our Heads: The Mental Demands of Modern Life*. Cambridge: Harvard University Press.

Kegan, R. and Lahey, L.L. (2001) *How the Way We Talk Can Change the Way We Work: Seven Languages for Transformation*. San Francisco: Jossey-Bass.

Kets de Vries, M.F.R. (2001) *The Leadership Mystique: An Owners Manual*. London: Prentice Hall.

Kiel, F., Rimmer, E., Williams, K. and Doyle, M. (1996) Coaching at the top, *Consulting Psychology Journal: Practice and Research*, 48(2): 67–77.

Kilburg, R.R. (1997) Coaching and executive character: core problems and basic approaches, *Consulting Psychology Journal: Practice and Research*, 49(4): 281–99.

Kilburg, R.R. (2000) *Executive Coaching: Developing Managerial Wisdom in a World of Chaos*. Washington: American Psychological Association.

Kilburg, R.R. (2001) Facilitating intervention adherence in executive coaching: a model and methods. *Consulting Psychology Journal: Practice and Research*, 53(4): 251–67.

Lee, G. (2003) *Leadership Coaching: From Personal Insight to Organisational Performance*. London: Chartered Institute of Personal Development.

Levinson, H. (1996) Executive coaching, *Consulting Psychology Journal: Practice and Research*, 48(2): 115–23.

Lewin, K. (1997) *Resolving Social Conflicts and Field Theory in Social Science*. Washington, DC: American Psychological Association.

Maccoby, M. (2000) Narcissistic leaders: the incredible pros, the inevitable cons, *The Harvard Business Review*, 78(1): 69–77.

Modoono, S.A. (2002) The executive coach self-assessment inventory, *Consulting Psychology Journal: Practice and Research*, 54(1): 43.

Nevis, E.C. (1987) *Organizational Consulting: A Gestalt Approach*. New York: Gardner Press.

Nevis, E.C. (1991) *Gestalt Therapy and Organization Development: A Historical Perspective, 1930–1966*. Hillsdale: The Analytic Press.

O'Neill, M.B. (2000) *Executive Coaching with Backbone and Heart: A Systems Approach to Engaging Leaders with their Challenges*. San Francisco: Jossey-Bass.

Peltier, B. (2001) *The Psychology of Executive Coaching: Theory and Application*. New York: Brunner-Routledge.

Perls, F.S. (1969) *Gestalt Therapy Verbatim*. Moab: Real People Press.

Polster, E. and Polster, M. (1973) *Gestalt Therapy Integrated*. New York: Brunner/ Mazel.

Prochaska, J.O., Norcross, J.C., DiClemente, C. (1994) *Changing for Good*. New York: William Morrow.

Proctor, B. (1986) Supervision: a co-operative exercise in accountability, in M. Marken and M. Payne (eds) *Enabling and Ensuring*. Leicester: National Youth Bureau and Council for Education and training in Youth and Community Work.

Rogers, C. (1961) *On Becoming a Person*. Boston: Houghton Mifflin.

Rogers, J. (2004) *Coaching Skills: A Handbook*. Maidenhead: Open University Press.

Skiffington, S. and Zeus, P. (2003) *Behavioural Coaching: How to Build Sustainable Personal and Organizational Strength*. North Ryde: McGraw-Hill.

Spencer Singer, B. (2001) *Recovering Executives at Risk of Derailing*. Durango: Lore International Institute.

Sperry, L. (2004) *Executive Coaching: The Essential Guide for Mental Health Professionals*. Hove: Brunner-Routledge.

Tobias, L.L. (1990) *Psychological Consulting To Management: A Clinician's Perspective*. New York: Brunner/Mazel.

Tobias, L.L. (1996) Coaching executives. *Consulting Psychology Journal: Practice and Research*, 48(2): 87–95.

Wasylyshyn, K.M. (2003) Executive coaching: an outcome study, *Consulting Psychology Journal: Practice and Research*, 55(2): 94–106.

Wheeler, G. and Backman, S. (1994) *On Intimate Ground: A Gestalt Approach to Working With Couples*. San Francisco: Jossey-Bass.

Zeus, P. and Skiffington, S. (2000) *The Complete Guide to Coaching at Work*. Roseville: McGraw-Hill.

Zinker, J.C. (1994) *In Search of Food Form: Gestalt Therapy with Couples and Families*. San Francisco: Jossey-Bass.

Index